MAKING A DIFFERENCE:

Reflections From Political Life

To Dancie,
with Best Wishes,
Kevin
September, 2008

MAKING A DIFFERENCE:

Reflections From Political Life

ERIC CLINE

thistledown press

Thistledown Press Ltd.
633 Main Street, Saskatoon, SK   S7H 0J8
www.thistledownpress.com

Library and Archives Canada Cataloguing in Publication
Cline, Eric, 1955–
Making a difference : reflections from political life / Eric Cline.
ISBN 978-1-897235-45-4
1. Cline, Eric, 1955–. 2. Cabinet ministers—Saskatchewan—Biography. 3. Saskatchewan. Legislative Assembly—Biography. 4. Legislators—Saskatchewan—Biography. 5. Saskatchewan—Politics and government—1991–. 6. Politicians—Saskatchewan—Biography.
I. Title.
FC3528.1.C55A3 2008   971.24′03092   C2008-904519-X

Publisher Cataloging-in-Publication Data (U.S)
(Library of Congress Standards)
Cline, Eric, 1955-
Making a difference: reflections from political life / Eric Cline
[225] p. : cm.
Summary: This memoir of Saskatchewan political maverick Eric Cline positively depicts his 17 year run as legal advisor and elected official during some of the province's most tumultuous years.
ISBN: 978-1-897235-45-4 (pbk.)
1. Cline, Eric, 1955– . 2. Saskatchewan—Politics and government—20th century—Biography. I. Title.
971.2403092 [B] dc22   F1072.C65 2009

Author photograph by Rosanna Parry
Cover and book design by Jackie Forrie
Printed and bound in Canada

10 9 8 7 6 5 4 3 2 1

Canada Council   Conseil des Arts
for the Arts   du Canada

SASKATCHEWAN
ARTS BOARD

Canadian   Patrimoine
Heritage   canadien

Thistledown Press gratefully acknowledges the financial assistance of the Canada Council for the Arts, the Saskatchewan Arts Board, and the Government of Canada through the Book Publishing Industry Development Program for its publishing program.

ACKNOWLEDGEMENTS

In this book I reflect on some of the policies, events and personalities I encountered in politics. For assistance in its preparation, I thank my typist Val Makela, and my wife Pauline Melis for her suggestions, patience, and loving support.

Eric Cline
Saskatoon, 2008

CONTENTS

The Political Terrain

A PLACE OF GRAND VISIONS AND BOLD INTENTIONS, yet underlying insecurity resulting from the experience of sudden and unpredictable hardship; liberal instincts contending with a tendency toward social conservatism; co-operative spirit, born of necessity, present in a strongly independent people: Saskatchewan contains all of these contradictions. It should come as no surprise that the province's competing impulses have produced strong politicians of the left and right, and a clash of political ideals, which has resonated more loudly than elsewhere in Canada.

Tommy Douglas was, in his day, either a saint or a devil, depending on who was doing the talking, and the same can probably be said of Ross Thatcher on the other side.

Growing up in Saskatchewan meant listening to political debates, which do not just involve traditional family loyalties, but also typically, at their core, arise from competing visions or values. People interested in public service through politics in Saskatchewan must eventually choose between the social democratic tradition of the CCF-NDP and the current party of the right, Liberal, Conservative or otherwise. Listening to my parents and our neighbours as a young person, I decided early on that I was a New Democrat.

Spring 1990 was a time of decision for me. I was a partner in one of the larger Saskatoon law firms, and, at the risk of sounding immodest, I was successful and becoming increasingly involved with growing my legal practice. But I had always been interested in politics, and involved in the Saskatchewan New Democratic Party since teenage years.

The people of the province had already decided that they would defeat the perceived incompetent and corrupt government led since 1982 by Premier Grant Devine. Huge annual deficits had allowed public debt to mushroom to the point where the once straight "A" credit ratings Saskatchewan had earned were gone, replaced with about the lowest ratings in Canada. Saskatchewan's once proud bond issues had the status of junk bonds. Theft and fraud by elected politicians eventually led to many criminal charges, convictions and jail sentences. The economy floundered. People had given up on the idea that Conservative government would get Saskatchewan growing. The only question was when the election would be called. The last vote, won by the NDP in October 1986, had resulted in a majority Progressive Conservative government due to the way in which the constituency boundaries were drawn. The less-populated rural seats favoured the Conservatives. Hence, fewer votes resulted in more seats for them. The Blakeney government of the 1970's had put an end to rigging the boundaries by allowing an independent commission to draw up seats of equal population, a practice abandoned by Devine but eventually restored by the Romanow government in the early 1990's.

As a lawyer and a political activist, various people had asked me from time to time if I would take a serious run at politics. As a nineteen-year-old student in 1975, at the request of the local party executive, I had allowed my name to stand in Regina South as a "paper" candidate. These are people who run in hopeless seats to fill out the slate. At that time, there was no hope of winning the Liberal stronghold of Regina South, won in 1975 by the able Stuart Cameron, who went on to become a judge of the Saskatchewan Court of Appeal and someone whom I came to know and respect. My campaign manager was Frank Quennell, who eventually became minister of Justice. We had many laughs as we tilted at windmills and, overall, it was fun and taught me that I could survive political battles.

A strong desire to beat the Devine Conservatives, coupled with a life-long interest in politics and a desire to serve the public had me pondering another run fifteen years later. This time, however, if I ran, I would run to win.

As it was, the Conservatives had redrawn the boundaries for the expected election. They were trying to create as many rural seats as possible. New Democrats were busy organizing nominating meetings to get candidates into place for an election that they knew should come soon. Historically votes in Saskatchewan are every four years, and often come in the early summer. So, an election might have been expected for June 1990. In fact, the election was ultimately held on October 21, 1991, more than a year later, and five years after the 1986 vote. But in the spring of 1990, we had to be ready for a vote at any time.

In October 1985 my wife Pauline Melis and I had moved into the Saskatoon neighbourhood of Massey Place, quite near where I grew up. We joined the NDP organization of

Bob Mitchell, who became our MLA in October the next year. He was also one of my law partners. By 1990, with the new boundaries, our house was located in a new riding called Saskatoon Idylwyld which stretched from the River Heights neighbourhood along the South Saskatchewan River all the way to the west end of Saskatoon. Although largely a "blue collar" constituency, because of its size it contained both affluent neighbourhoods such as River Heights and lower income neighbourhoods like Mayfair, Woodlawn and McNab Park. It was the second largest riding in the Province, with twice as many people in it as most rural ridings. This inequality of numbers was one of many examples of what I came to call "Tory Math." They always got their numbers wrong. Projected budget deficits could be out by hundreds of millions of dollars.

There was no incumbent MLA for Saskatoon Idylwyld. Ray Meiklejohn, a Tory cabinet minister, represented a large part of it. He would run in the new constituency of River Heights, more affluent and possibly safe territory for the Tories. Ultimately, he went down to defeat at the hands of the able and personable Carol Teichrob, a seasoned veteran of rural municipal politics who went on to serve two terms as a valued MLA and cabinet minister. Of course, if there had been any seat where Ray Meiklejohn could have succeeded, it would have been the new River Heights, so it was the best strategy for the Conservatives, albeit a losing one.

Anne Smart, MLA for Saskatoon Centre, elected in 1986, had represented a small part of the Idylwyld riding. Her riding was done away with by redistribution. John Brockelbank MLA represented most of the new Saskatoon Westmount that absorbed her area, and it was assumed he would run there.

Anne would therefore contest Saskatoon Idylwyld, the new seat. In fact, unknown to her, Saskatoon Westmount, which took in most of her territory, would not be contested by John Brockelbank, in favour of whom she had bowed out. Plans were already afoot for John to step down and Janice MacKinnon to step up to the plate while the battle for the Idylwyld nomination was on. Anne was unaware of this. It was a closely guarded secret that few people knew. The plan was for Janice to be acclaimed after the shortest possible notice of meeting, with no time for another candidate to come forward.

Gordon Gunoff, a plainspoken and interesting personality, had come close to defeating Ray Meiklejohn in 1986 in the old Saskatoon Mayfair riding. He had worked hard and had more of a connection to the area, as a long-time resident, than Anne Smart did. I believed Gordon deserved his shot at the new seat of Saskatoon Idylwyld. Anne believed Gordon was not a strong candidate and that she could come in and beat him for the nomination. She was probably underestimating Gordon, who is an aggressive campaigner. I decided I would support Gordon's bid to run again rather than running myself. I would make myself available to the new government in some other supportive role. But, the political landscape can quickly change, and it was about to do so.

Along with other legal colleagues, I had been providing the NDP caucus with free legal advice and analysis for several years. I knew that there were several ways I could help and support a new government without standing for election. This could involve working with the party to keep the political organization strong, providing advice, or actually working for government. I was close enough to many major players in the NDP, such as Roy Romanow and Bob Mitchell, to be present at discussions of political strategy. Opposition parties often simply have to wait for governments to "defeat themselves." This was very true in the case of the Devine Conservatives. The public was not just "tired" of them, or "in the mood for a change"; they were downright hostile toward the Conservatives. They sensed that there was incompetence in government, if not corruption. They were proved right when it was eventually revealed that criminal charges were being laid against several Conservative politicians. They knew the finances were in a mess, and the economy was weak. Grant Devine's plea to the public of "don't compare me to perfection" was met by howls of derisive laughter. As if anyone would! So, the strategy of the NDP was two-fold. First, to avoid saying anything that would turn any particular group off, thereby ensuring their annoyance continued to be solely directed at the governing Conservatives. Second, to prepare the public for the fact that there was a mess to be cleaned up, and to condition them to the reality that the new NDP government could not initially embark on new programs. Rather, the job of the new government was to restore fiscal integrity and honesty in government. In the common vernacular of the NDP, it was stated that Saskatchewan needed to "open the books, and jail the crooks."

Nomination and Intimidation

I WAS DETERMINED TO ACT TO HELP DEFEAT the Conservatives. Not only was I a committed social democrat and opponent of right-wing ideology, but also I believed that Devine was wrecking the province fiscally and, therefore, ultimately economically. People cannot succeed and thrive in an unstable fiscal and tax environment. I was angered at Conservative attempts to privatize crown corporations like SaskEnergy. I find nothing offensive about the idea that people can equally own the utilities they rely upon, and share the benefits they generate. Their privatization agenda, coupled with huge gifts to the private sector, including the giant forest products company Weyerhaeuser, bothered me a great deal. Their sell-off of the Potash Corporation and the Prince Albert Pulp Mill at the bottom of the market demonstrated complete disregard of the public good, and contempt for the institution of government itself.

At the age of thirty-five, I was quite willing to interrupt my legal career to assist Roy Romanow and the New Democrats. Aside from my political leanings, I had come to know and respect Roy as a person as much as a party leader. Though, while he was still in elected office, Roy Romanow was sometimes portrayed by the Saskatchewan media as arrogant and distant from the concerns and needs of ordinary people, anyone who knows Roy knows that nothing could be further from the truth. Highly intelligent, sometimes argumentative, provocative and single-minded in his pursuits, Roy is a thoroughly decent, honest and passionate Canadian and Saskatchewanian who never forgot his roots. He always pursued the public interest and, most telling to me, invariably came to forgive and extend the olive branch to those who opposed him and, in some cases, betrayed him over the years, both inside and outside the party.

After twelve years of legal work, I had also found myself thinking that there was more to life than the practice of law. While I knew I could practice law for another thirty years, make money and retire, I thought there had to be more. I had certainly been fortunate in my career choice. I articled to Ed Gosselin, who become a Provincial Court judge, and to Silas E. Halyk, QC who, along with Gerald N. Allbright, QC, now a Queen's Bench judge, became trusted mentors and friends.

But, I wanted to do more. I felt that I wanted to make a difference in a way that simply practicing law did not afford me. A desire to devote part of my life to public service drove me toward a greater political commitment.

Becoming a member of the new Saskatoon Idylwyld constituency executive, I developed misgivings about our "buddy" MLA, as the NDP had named Anne Smart. A "buddy" is an MLA from another constituency who serves as a contact with constituencies represented by another party. Gordon Gunoff had decided not to contest the nomination in Saskatoon Idylwyld after all. This was a surprise to me. I think he was just tired of political infighting. Opposing a sitting

MLA is frowned upon. I toyed with the idea of running, since I had both an interest and deep roots in the area, but thought better of it given that Anne was a new MLA. I generally feel that every MLA deserves a second term. As well, it was not common to challenge sitting members for nomination.

But I still had misgivings about Anne's judgment and ability to relate to people. The constituency network itself seemed disorganized, with only about 119 paid up members, a small number for a large riding with much NDP support. It was also still in debt from the past election. The executive was small and largely run out of Anne's MLA office in downtown Saskatoon, away from the riding. All politics is local, and strong organizations rely on people "on the ground", not paid politicians and staff. Also, I had heard several party members raise questions about Anne's effectiveness as an MLA.

It has been a blessing and a curse for me, in personal and political life, that I tend to speak my mind and do not back away from an argument. It was not long before I came to feel unwelcome at the meetings of the Saskatoon Idylwyld constituency executive, and sometimes clashed with Anne and her supporters.

In February 1990, shortly after our riding was formed, we held an executive meeting at which we discussed when to hold a nomination convention to select a candidate. Anne and her supporters wanted an early date. Of course, from their point of view, the then small number of card-carrying members could come together, as is sometimes the case, and rubber-stamp the pre-ordained, and only, candidate. Choosing the date for a nomination often involves candidates "jockeying" for position. Early candidates want an early date to prevent others from joining the race and bringing in people who may vote for the newer candidates.

During the discussion, I said that a later date would permit us to get more paid up members, get better organized and perhaps have a contested nomination to increase interest. I had not spoken long, and, while in mid-sentence, Anne Smart turned to me in anger. "Would you please finish. Say your speech, and then the rest of us will have our say."

I was stunned. I felt that I had been slapped in the face, and I felt humiliated in front of the ten or so people present. An elected person had never spoken me to like this. I was quiet for the rest of the evening, because I felt like an outsider, someone not to be "included" in the like-minded group. Anne probably reacted defensively because she felt threatened in her position as MLA, a position she enjoyed. She likely also felt vulnerable in a new constituency. These are normal feelings in politics, where paranoia is not uncommon. Anne has many fine qualities, but the pressure-cooker environment of politics can bring out edginess.

Anne or her supporters must have sensed that she had inappropriately lost her cool at the meeting. The next day, her partner Larry Mullen phoned Terry Stevens, then Director of the United Steelworkers' Saskatoon office. Terry was a respected trade union leader and a long-time friend of mine. Larry apparently called Terry to report the incident with Anne. Not knowing me well, he asked Terry whether I was the sort of person who would forget about it or whether I would "do something." Terry told me that he advised Larry that he felt I was not a vindictive person, but that I had been politically active in the NDP for a long time, and I might decide to support someone other than Anne.

This incident confirmed my existing inclination that I did not want Anne Smart representing me and my neighbours in the legislature. I phoned my good friend and long-time political co-worker and confidante, Angie Fergusson. If ever there was a savvy and wise political organizer, it is Angie. I told her I was thinking of seeking the NDP nomination in the new constituency of Saskatoon Idylwyld and wanted her opinion. She laughed out loud, vigorously. Not sure what to make of that, I listened to her advice. She told me to seek the opinions of politically experienced, long-time NDP members in the riding. She said I should start with George Semeniuk, long-time veteran union activist, NDP stalwart and west-side resident. She said I should get back to her with their responses and she would offer further advice. I am quite sure she felt they would tell me not to challenge an incumbent MLA, and if so, she would then affirm that advice and I would get on with my life.

Having arranged to meet George Semeniuk for coffee, I told him what I was thinking. He immediately offered his encouragement and support. Similar visits to long-time respected Mayfair resident and eventual close friend, Lil Hyland, retired Fire Marshall Don Zolmer and his wife Mary Lynn, NDP activist Barb Macnab and her sister Bev Wilson, former candidate Gordon Gunoff and several others produced similar responses. I had lots of support. Duly reporting this response back to Angie, as promised, she laughed again. What was with this woman? She, too, offered her support, and the race was on. Well, nearly on.

There was the matter of getting agreement from my wife, Pauline. She remained unenthusiastic about the proposal, arguing that to take on a sitting MLA would be divisive, could become controversial and even "ugly". Little did I know how right she was. Nevertheless, Pauline said that if this is what I wanted to do with my life, if this is something that I would enjoy, I had her blessing. Now, the race was on.

Shortly thereafter, it was nearly off. Having made my candidacy known, I attended another meeting of the Idylwyld NDP executive. They were not amused. I am sure others have been at gatherings where nothing in particular is actually said, but they felt "shunned". That is how I felt. The meeting was tense. And, Pauline was right. The challenge would be divisive in our constituency and party. The mood of the meeting suggested to me that it could get "ugly". Feeling unwelcome and depressed after the meeting, I arrived home about 10:00 in the evening and found Pauline sitting in bed, reading.

I told her she was right, recounted the meeting and that I had decided life was too short for this kind of heartache and strife. If people were going to be hostile to me, I was out of the race. It was not too late to bow out and call it off. I was pretty thin-skinned, something politics would eventually change. My inclination, at least at that moment, was to avoid conflict that might make me uncomfortable.

At that, Pauline did something that surprises me today, almost exactly eighteen years later. She sat up in bed, and looked at me standing beside her. "Oh, big-time politician," she said. "You announced your candidacy a few days ago, and the first time some people are rude to you, you back out! Get used to it! You are going to have a lot of disputes in politics. It goes with the territory. So get at it."

Now, there I was thinking she would welcome my swift and cautious retreat. Actually, anything that happened didn't faze her, because she expected the unexpected, both in politics and in life. Pauline and her twin sister, her only sibling, had lost both parents by the age of twelve. They had been on their own since moving to Saskatoon at the age of sixteen. In her own way, she was much less naive than I was. Politically, she was from a long-time CCF-NDP family, and I was not. She gave me my marching orders. I had committed to running, so I was in. We agreed that I should "toughen up" and see my decision through.

As I said, my skin then was not very thick, not as thick as it became reading or hearing uncharitable comments about me in my life as a politician. I really was not used to being criticized in public. It made me cringe and depressed me. I thought it is likely why ninety-nine percent of people would never run for office. It is understandable. People do not want to be criticized in public. But, criticism is part of the political game. It is part of living in a free and democratic society. And, as a politician, it is part of being human. Sometimes we make mistakes. We can be right, and we can be wrong, or be seen to be wrong, in any event. In politics, you need to be prepared to accept the criticism that naturally comes with it. You come to realize that most people don't pay much attention to political criticism anyway. Most people are busy with their own lives — making a living and raising their kids. They don't have time to follow political debates. The ones who pay attention usually have their own political opinions, they have seen it all before, and they take political commentary with a grain of salt.

My battle for the May 1990 NDP nomination in Saskatoon Idylwyld was divisive, but also decisive. In the end, some 600 delegates and observers packed the Saskatoon Union Centre to nominate their candidate. Word of a hotly-contested nomination turned out an interested crowd. I won by a 2-to-1 margin. After the win, many accusations of "dirty tricks" were levelled at my team, and me, as is sometimes the case after a nominating convention. For example, we had sold about 350 new memberships, but did not share the names with the party office and, therefore, my opponent, until the deadline for turning in memberships, which was two weeks before the nominating meeting. This is a common practice in contested nominations, but angered the other side, which had to scramble to visit these people in a few weeks. They had only sold a handful of new memberships; the reality is they were just "out organized" and taken by surprise. In their minds, they were unfairly ambushed. There were also allegations that some of the new members had not paid for their own memberships. These allegations were extensively investigated and found to be unsubstantiated. Although there were calls to overturn the vote, when the dust settled the result was clear and I was on the road to a political life.

It had been a hotly contested nomination and I was a bit shell-shocked by the whole experience. Friends like Bob and Sandy Mitchell and Michael Finley and Anne Doucette provided much advice and support during what became a difficult time. I was not sleeping at night because of media attention to Anne's "dirty tricks" allegations. I was very embarrassed by the allegations, but knew I could not run away, or turn back.

While seeking the nomination for Idylwyld taught me first-hand that politics could be an ugly business, I had been introduced to its darker side earlier in my life. In 1977, when I was a law student, I was asked by my friend Angie Fergusson to come and help out in the Pelly by-election, where Norman Lusney was running to replace the late NDP member Leonard Larson who had died in office. It was summer vacation, so I agreed to go.

While working on the by-election, some NDP workers were staying at Madge Lake at some cabins and it turned out that some Conservative organizers were staying there too.

One night, a woman was sexually assaulted in the park, and two women from the NDP campaign drove her to the hospital in Kamsack. She told them that she was a worker for the Conservatives in the by-election, there had been drinking, and another Conservative worker had assaulted her. The NDP women, whom I knew, comforted her as best they could and made sure she got help at the hospital.

The next morning, the NDP campaign workers talked about the incident. We decided we would say nothing. If there was to be a complaint to the police, it should come from the woman. If she wouldn't complain herself, how could we? The police would require her co-operation. In a far lesser consideration, we also decided we did not wish to win the by-election by displaying the Conservatives' dirty linen in public and that we would keep our mouths shut about it, which we did.

Two years later, in 1979, while I was still a law student, two Conservative lawyers in Saskatoon asked me to come to their office. Naively, and therefore without a witness, I did so. They asked for a conversation, and I had no reason to be wary. When I arrived, they told me that they wanted certain information about a particular incident that I saw at once to be an attempt to embarrass a Saskatoon NDP MLA. They said they knew I was at Madge Lake when a sexual assault had taken place, and were insinuating that I had something to do with it. They said they would report me to the police and Law Society, and then again asked for information about the MLA concerning a subject I knew nothing about.

I was twenty-three years old and naive, but a good law student. I knew enough to tell them that if they ever tried to accuse me of anything about the Madge Lake incident, I would sue them for defamation of character and/or malicious prosecution and I walked out. I immediately told my law school friend, Stephen Carter, now a Provincial Court judge, what had happened. He, in turn, told his father, Roger Carter, QC, the former Dean of Law. Roger was outraged and he felt I should go and see David Kaiser, now also a Provincial Court judge and his partners Ken Walker and Robert Walker, QC, a former Attorney-General. I went to see them and described the incident. They advised that there was nothing further that could be done unless the Conservative lawyers tried something further. I thought the incident would end there.

Eleven years later, in the spring of 1990, I was nominated as an NDP candidate. Once again the ugly side of politics made itself evident. A former Conservative MLA went to see NDP leader Roy Romanow. He told Roy that his new candidate had been present when a sexual assault had occurred at Madge Lake and this would soon be "the word on the street."

Roy didn't believe a word of it, but, of course, had to tell me that the conversation had happened. I was concerned, not because I thought I could ever be connected to a crime, but because it sounded like the Conservatives were going to attempt to smear the NDP and me in the run-up to the impending election. I was sick with worry, as anyone would be. I imagined that the allegations would soon be circulated and what would I do? Lawsuits and criminal proceedings take a long time, and we would never have the matter dealt with before the election. Should I withdraw as a candidate to save us all the embarrassment and, most importantly, to protect the party? These kinds of allegations, even if unfounded, can hurt entire political parties and affect the outcome of elections.

I decided to go and talk to my articling principal and mentor, Silas E. Halyk, QC, one of the best lawyers in Canada.

I explained all that had occurred, including the events at Madge Lake, the attempt to scare information out of me when I was a law student, and now the attempt to intimidate me as an NDP candidate. I told him I was worried sick about it.

Si just told me to stop worrying. First of all, he found the allegation preposterous. He said that they could not use the criminal justice system for political ends. The Crown prosecutors are independent and would not allow it. Furthermore, he thought that if they persisted, they themselves could be charged with criminal defamation. He said to just forget about it and get on with things. Coming from someone as knowledgeable and experienced as Si Halyk, I put the matter out of my mind.

Later, at a public meeting, I ran into the former Conservative MLA who had spoken to Roy Romanow. I gave him a piece of my mind about what he had tried to do, and told him that if he ever said anything about me like that again, I would sue him for every penny he had. Ironically, though not surprisingly, he was later charged and convicted for fraud.

I do not wish to leave the impression that I run around threatening to sue people for defamation on a frequent basis. In fact, I think these two incidents, one in 1979 and the next in 1990, were the only times I ever did threaten to sue someone over something they said. I certainly have felt over the years that sometimes words were said about me that were not completely accurate, and some were outright insulting and untrue. These, however, were not politically inspired allegations of vicious and despicable criminal behaviour. There are limits to what a person should be prepared to put up with, and with respect to these particular incidents, if they had persisted, I certainly would have taken them to court. As mentioned, politics can be an ugly business, but it can also be an extremely rewarding connection to people. In May 1990, I was still busy attending to my legal practice and getting a political organization together. I needed to get on with the job of getting elected.

In any political organization or campaign, many, many people become involved. These people are like a large extended family to the candidate. They are decent, hard-working people trying to participate in the democratic process. They truly believe in what they are doing, and that it helps to ensure a decent life for their children and their community. Every political party has many people who are dedicated and sincere volunteers. For me, they are too numerous to mention. But, they are frequently in my thoughts when I think about political life. Many of them are close personal friends. My first task in getting elected was to secure that extended family, and create an organization that would be effective and run smoothly — in essence, to create a winning team.

Connecting With the Constituency

THE ELECTION OF OCTOBER 21, 1991 CAME upon us for the very simple reason that it could not be postponed any longer. The Conservative government had been operating on special warrants for many months, afraid to summon the legislature, afraid of the public, afraid of the opposition NDP. No budget had been passed for the 1991-92 fiscal year, Premier Devine having shut down the legislative assembly after Grant Hodgins, minister of Environment and Government House Leader, resigned on June 17, 1991 before the budget could be passed. He stated that he could not support Devine's "Fair Share" Program, which would have distributed the public servants living and working in Regina throughout the province.

Although we had no doubt Saskatoon Idylwyld would go NDP, I was determined that I would campaign hard and get to know as many constituents as I could. I went "door knocking" from the time of my nomination in May 1990 until Election Day in October 1991, a period of seventeen months. One would assume that, in that time, a candidate would get to every doorstep. I likely did, but I soon discovered that I was the world's slowest canvasser. Like my parents and most of my family, I love to meet and visit with people. Also, I wanted to connect with the people I was to represent in the legislature. I found it phoney and presumptuous to simply shake hands at the doorstep while quickly introducing myself. I wanted to take the time to actually discuss issues and concerns, and to know what people were thinking. It takes a long time to do this, but when you do, you develop a lot of good connections in the community, a personal following and a lot of committed supporters.

I was always advised by my cousin Dave Morgan and NDP organizers to close my visits with voters by saying, "I hope I can count on your support," but I have never done this, feeling that it makes the voter uncomfortable by putting him or her on the spot. I would sooner leave them to make up their own minds, hoping that I had left a favourable impression. A successful door-knocking strategy, in my opinion, involves being real with people, letting them know that politicians can be sincere and can relate to their concerns.

It doesn't take long to realize, meeting people, that there really is a "general public". That is, while there are political parties and interest groups like the Chamber of Commerce and the trade union movement, and while there are the media and various groups which have views, there is a wider, more general "public" view — the Joes and Marthas of the world with no affiliation to any organized interest coalition who nevertheless are the largest and most important group out there. The Joes and Marthas of the world are the ones politicians should seek to represent.

I always tried to let this strategy guide me during my years as a representative of the people. One incident comes immediately to mind. Years after the 1991 election in which I was first elected, during the 2003 election there was an all-party debate at the Saskatoon Construction Association. I was representing the NDP, and Don Morgan was representing the opposition Saskatchewan Party. Both the Liberal leader David Karwacki and his brother Grant represented the Liberal Party. David had to leave halfway through the debate and Grant stepped up to replace him. (The Karwacki brothers are apparently interchangeable.)

The debate at the Saskatoon Construction Association was largely a love-in for the opposition Saskatchewan Party. It never ceases to amaze me that no matter how good the economy is under the NDP, there are certain business groups that invariably and blindly long for the days of recession they usually get under Conservative government. One of the construction business people present thought he would put me on the spot by challenging me. "When are you finally going to represent our interests?" he demanded of me. "Never," I replied. That seemed to get their attention. "I don't represent you. I don't represent the Chamber of Commerce. I don't represent the Saskatchewan Federation of Labour. I represent the public."

I went on to explain that sometimes we made decisions in government that annoyed the business community, and sometimes we annoyed the labour community. Nevertheless, it was our job to try to determine what we thought was in the public interest, and to act accordingly. Although this incident of the all-party debate was years later, in my first bid to win an election in 1991, I had formed a voter strategy and philosophy that would serve me well through the years. I tried to avoid promises to vested interest groups, and, in determining the public interest, I always asked myself what Joe and Martha would think.

Reality Sinks In

THE NDP CAME TO GOVERNMENT IN 1991 with a resounding victory, winning fifty-five of sixty-six seats that were available at that time. Voter turnout in 1991 was very high. Well over eighty percent of the people voted, which often means a change of government. The NDP won over fifty percent of the vote, which is not that common in a three-party system. But rather than feeling euphoric about the win, I felt the hard work was just about to begin.

Like other MLAs I have talked to, I felt in awe, almost overwhelmed, the first time I sat in the large, ornate legislative chamber. The ghosts of political greats like Walter Scott, Tommy Douglas and Allan Blakeney make one question one's own qualifications to be there. It was, however, reassuring to be guided by veterans like Ned Shillington and Ed Tchorzewski. Roy Romanow, of course, was the acknowledged master in the house.

Many lasting friendships arise in politics among party members and especially amongst the MLAs. My seatmate, Armand Roy, was MLA for Kinistino. He was a farmer, also newly elected, and we became close friends. We were among a handful of "thirty-something" newly elected MLAs. We both discovered that we had the same uncertainties about our roles, instincts and so on. It is great to have a "sounding board" colleague. You share a lot of laughs with your seatmate as you figure things out together. Unfortunately, Armand was defeated in the 1995 election, along with many rural NDP MLAs. They were casualties of the Romanow government's attempts to balance the budget, reform health care and diversify agriculture. These reforms involved conversion of fifty hospitals to health clinics and the cancellation of the farmers' GRIP program, which paid farmers hundreds of millions of dollars per year to grow wheat the world market didn't want.

In 1991, I don't think many of us new MLAs, unlike veterans like Roy Romanow and Ed Tchorzewski, really knew what we were getting into. Assuming the reins of power from Grant Devine was quite a challenge. What a mess! The financial situation was worse than anyone expected, which probably explains why no budget had been presented to the legislature for a few years. Today, it is unthinkable that a government of Saskatchewan would operate without a budget.

In the days of Devine, there were no regular meetings of the Treasury Board, which is the most important instrument of government to keep finances on track. There were no timely public accounts released after year-end. There were no mid-year financial statements, let alone quarterly financial statements. In the end, the Devine government did not get away with this. Most voters knew something was seriously wrong when a government did not even operate on a budget. The Romanow NDP brought in mid-year financial statements, then quarterly statements, regular Treasury Board oversight of spending, and timely budgets.

Celebration of political victory in 1991 quickly gave way to the grim reality of governing Saskatchewan. Grim due to a nearly billion-dollar deficit on an approximately five-billion dollar budget: scandalous and unsustainable. That state of economics meant that those who voted NDP out of a belief that the NDP could spend on a variety of social programs would be disappointed. Some would quickly abandon the party, while others accepted that the new government had to repair the fiscal situation it inherited before embarking on new spending. Remembering that situation, when I heard Conservative premier-elect Brad Wall complain in 2007 that the outgoing NDP government only left him with about $1.4 billion in the bank — the highest ever inherited by an incoming government — I didn't know whether to laugh or cry, but finally I laughed anyway. (I do hope Premier Wall can manage somehow: he can always call Roy Romanow for advice!)

The fact of the matter is that, from 1991 to 1993, Saskatchewan was on the verge of bankruptcy. Any government must finance its operations through the sale of bonds to ensure cash flow. Saskatchewan had gone from over 120 investment houses that would invest clients' money in Saskatchewan to around twenty, and that number was dwindling. Those that did buy saw our bonds as junk bonds, for which they charge higher interest payments because of the perceived risk that you might not be able to pay the money back.

Drastic times call for drastic measures. New Premier Romanow appointed his "war cabinet" of ten members, half the usual size. It was armed with the responsibility, first, to get Saskatchewan's fiscal house in order. This task fell mainly to veteran MLA and former Finance Minister Ed Tchorzewski.

From November 1991 to January 1993, Ed had the tough job of leading the decision-making process that created the foundation for the balanced budget achieved under Finance Minister Janice MacKinnon in the spring of 1994. The late John Penner, MLA for Swift Current, ably assisted Ed. John was one of the hardest workers and a true gentleman of politics. He served as minister of Crown Investments and associate Finance minister. For health reasons, he did not seek re-election in 1995 and was replaced as Swift Current MLA by John Wall, another gentleman-teacher.

There is no question that Janice MacKinnon deserves much of the credit she has been given for her work in finance, but Ed Tchorzewski remains an unsung hero. Balanced budgets, like most things that matter, do not happen overnight. They happen because of plans made over the years, and Ed had to lay the foundation that allowed revenues to meet expenditures by 1994. Janice MacKinnon is a quick study, and was able to continue Ed's balanced budget plan when she became Finance minister in January 1993. She, and the province, benefitted greatly from the fact that so much heavy lifting had been done by Ed.

The period November 1991 to May 1992, when the Romanow government produced its first budget, was a time when the entire caucus agonized over the cutbacks and tax increases that simply had to occur to balance the budget. Incidentally, there never was a budget for 1991-92, which must be an historical first. The NDP did produce a Financial Statement in late 1991, but by then it was too far into the fiscal year to present a budget. A budget is a document that looks forward to the year ahead. Two-thirds of the fiscal year had already gone by when Grant Devine left office in early November 1991.

The return of the NDP to government in 1991 ushered in a period of tough decision making in Saskatchewan politics. Critics included those on the left who could not accept the actions government took to balance the budget. Those of us in the NDP caucus felt that, ultimately, if *we* didn't get the bankers off our backs, if twenty cents on the dollar went on interest payments (now more like seven cents on the dollar) how would we ever have the financial freedom to do what we all wanted to do? My colleagues and I were social democrats who came to politics and public life to equalize opportunities through public education, public health care and assistance to those in need. We did not enter public life to cut services back or to raise taxes for ordinary people.

But there was a bigger picture, and we became determined not to deviate from our task. Many critics urged us to let the province go bankrupt citing rationale like "It is not my debt. I didn't create it. Why should I have to pay for it?" I, and others, replied that, ultimately, only the taxpayers could pay for public debt. And, yes, Saskatchewan could hypothetically go bankrupt but that would likely mean the Bank of Canada would have to take control of our assets, and the crown corporations would have to be sold, no doubt at fire sale prices. Is that what they wanted?

It was also during this period that I came to realize that being a member of the opposition would be very easy. Governing was hard. As a new MLA, even with the overwhelming support of my constituents, I was not able to do what I really wanted including, for example, increasing education funding and decreasing taxes for ordinary people. In fact, I had to support policies and decision making that, taken in isolation, I didn't agree with. For example, I cringed at reducing funding for education — it is the most important public policy area on which you can spend money. But the overall target I did agree with. Along with my colleagues, I was prepared to support an approach that would lead to a balanced budget over the first term of the Romanow government.

It wasn't easy. Rancorous debates in caucus occurred. Neighbours who were friends and political supporters chastised me in my home riding about tax increases and cutbacks. Being a government MLA does not involve "being all things to all people". It involves tough choices.

Driving back to Saskatoon one Friday with colleague Pat Atkinson, I had to admit that I hadn't left the practice of law for this kind of heartache and acrimony. Pat had been a candidate since 1982, and an MLA since 1986. She was a left-wing idealist who nevertheless could face reality and accept decisions that had to be made. She understood how I felt, since she was also disappointed that we were unable at this time to do things we wanted to do. Pat is a dedicated and passionate individual. A popular Saskatoon MLA, Pat became the longest-serving female MLA in Saskatchewan's history. Though I enjoyed baiting Pat just to get her going, she became a trusted friend and, ultimately, my front-bench seatmate. (Was it just an accident that I sat to her right and she to my left?)

Regarding the early months of government, I was quite depressed for weeks about the fact that the public did not support our government's efforts to balance the budget. The polls had us lagging the opposition. What was the point of doing all this good work if people hated us? And to make matters worse, it appeared that we were going to lose the next election to the Liberals led by Lynda Haverstock.

I finally snapped out of my political depression sometime in the summer of 1992 when the opposition was busy keeping us in the legislature over cancellation of the GRIP program, a controversial subsidy directly supporting crop farm incomes. Having supper with Prince Albert MLA Eldon Lautermilch, I complained to him that I thought we were doing the right things, but the public hated it and would turf us out in the next election.

Eldon simply looked at me. "Maybe that's our job," he said. "Fix the financial situation. Get it done. Let the people do what they want."

I never worried about losing an election again. It was our job to do the right thing. Take the hits. But at the end of the day, go back to the basic fundamental question: What do you believe is in the public interest? Define that. Then try to do it. Stare the critics down. If you do what you think is right, and get thrown out of office, at least you can feel good about what you did while in government.

Towards the end of the first term of the Romanow NDP government, the tide of popular opinion turned in favour of the government. Buoyed by the balanced budget presented by Janice MacKinnon in the spring of 1994, with the full participation and support of her cabinet and caucus colleagues, the able leadership of Dwain Lingenfelter in the Economic Development portfolio, and an improving economy, Lynda Haverstock's and the Liberals' substantial lead in the polls began to dissipate. Coupled with a badly conceived and conducted 1995 Liberal election campaign, Premier Romanow's government was returned in the spring 1995 election.

The constituency boundaries were redrawn after the reinstatement of "representation by population". I was elected in the new constituency of Saskatoon Mount Royal, which I went on to represent for two terms, until it vanished with redistribution for the election of 2003. Happily, by 1995, friends and foes of the bitter 1990 nomination fight worked together to re-elect me as the NDP candidate. I had worked very hard to reach out to those who had not supported me for nomination in 1990. In my acceptance speech in May 1990, I had begun the process by saying that although some had not supported me that night, it was my intention "to make you proud to have me as your MLA." To many, I had succeeded, and by 1995 they were fully on board the campaign bus.

On Being A Constituency MLA

MANY BELIEVE THAT IT IS THE IMMEDIATE WISH of every newly elected, ambitious, young MLA to go into cabinet. This is often not the case, and was not the case with me. I found the decisions that the new government had to make daunting. I had neither the experience nor the toughness to answer for them. I was learning the ropes as an MLA. Anyone working with members of the legislature knows that the job is what you make of it. You can go along for the ride, or you can really work at it. The vast majority of MLAs, on both sides of the house, work hard.

There are many opportunities to serve in the legislature, and I began to make my mark as a member of cabinet's Legislative Review Committee. I was the caucus representative selected by my colleagues. This committee basically oversaw the government's legislative agenda. This committee must vet every bill or regulation proposed by a cabinet minister. It was a lot of work, but I enjoyed it.

Premier Romanow also asked me to sit on the legislature's Public Accounts Committee, and to become vice-chair in 1993. The Committee reviews the Provincial Auditor's annual or special reports on how government departments and agencies spend the public's money. It then makes recommendations to the Legislative Assembly on how to improve financial practices and accountability. An opposition MLA chairs it, but because the government has a majority on the Committee, control effectively rests with the vice-chair. During the Devine years, the Committee had been dominated by Conservative MLAs, and never did the job of bringing financial excesses to light. We were determined that this would not happen again. When Premier Romanow asked me, with the consent of previous Vice-Chair Harry Van Mulligan, to become vice-chair, he told me it would be good preparation for future cabinet responsibilities. Being vice-chair of Public Accounts also involved a lot of work, but I also enjoyed that challenge. I think my legal colleagues and some political colleagues always considered me a "workaholic" and, in some cases, a "hard-nosed pain-in-the-ass". This was likely true, but I always made the most of the responsibilities I was assigned.

Despite my increasing workload assignments, the most important part of my job was to represent the people of my constituency and others that came for help. My legal background and many community connections, as well as the fact that from 1991 to 1995 I was a "back bench" MLA, meant that I was often the person that members of the public in Saskatoon went to when they had some problem with government. All of my NDP colleagues from the west side of Saskatoon (Roy Romanow, Bob Mitchell, Janice MacKinnon and Carol Teichrob) served in the cabinet. This meant that I was often the one "on the ground" in Saskatoon to deal with the concerns of constituents, at least insofar as the west side was involved. Having given up my law partnership and practicing law only on a part-time basis, when I wasn't required in Regina for committee or legislative work, I devoted myself almost full-time to dealing with individual concerns. This involved long days at the constituency office, typically from 8:00 AM to 6:00 PM, and then back again after supper.

People come into MLA offices with all kinds of concerns. They deserve to be listened to, treated with respect and, except in those few cases where they are asking for improper favours, to be helped. Concerns involve being denied workers' compensation, denial of social assistance benefits, student loan problems, SGI removal of driver's license, disputes over value of car "totalled" in accident, disputes over who was at fault for an accident and, after "no fault" insurance, denial of benefits or of legal assistance. Being a lawyer meant that I received many inquiries from people who basically wanted to run their problem by a lawyer because they either could not afford one, or did not wish to pay for legal services.

Sometimes, people just need someone to listen to them. Amazingly, that is often what people really want and, if you give them a proper hearing they are much happier than they were on arrival. When the MLA is away from his or her office, the responsibility to administer the office and to be "front line" in meeting the public falls to the constituency assistant.

In my case, I had the benefit early on of Treena Dobson, a legal secretary, who came to be my constituency assistant. After she left, Lynda MacPherson ably assisted our constituents and me for a number of years and, after 1997, Donna Rederburg served in that capacity. Each assistant proved to be very capable. Each was liked and respected by constituents. Whether due to my ability to judge prospective employees or good luck, or both, I have been well served by my constituency assistants and my office always had a reputation for getting the job done for people. This was largely due to the people who assisted me in my office whose roles became all the more important after my appointment to cabinet following the 1995 election.

Being an MLA means that you have to advocate for constituents who are not getting a fair deal. On some occasions advocating for constituents could also lead to questionable attitudes on the part of the bureaucracy. Sometimes, departments and agencies feel that MLAs bringing constituents' plights to government amounts to "political interference". In fact, advocating for individuals who are not getting a fair shake from government is part of the MLA's job. If the MLA doesn't do it, the voters should fire him or her.

One amusing incident of bureaucratic resistance related to a constituent who was a long-time heavy equipment operator and, as a result, lost most of his hearing. His doctor and audiologist prescribed a certain type of hearing aid for his hearing loss. The Workers' Compensation Board told him, and later me, that he couldn't have the hearing aid unless the need for it arose from a particular "medical condition". The Board said the medical people hadn't outlined any "medical condition". The man was perplexed because he couldn't hear, the doctor wrote that he couldn't hear, and he felt this was a "medical condition". So did I.

I phoned the Workers' Compensation Board but the person told me that he had to have a "medical condition". I said he did: "He can't hear."

"Yes," the Board employee said, "we know he can't hear but it must be associated with a medical condition."

"He can't hear," I repeated. "That is a medical condition." And so it went. Finally, I just phoned the Chair of the Board and, the next day, the man got his hearing aid. I am sure the Board worker saw this as some kind of inappropriate "political interference". It is not. The man couldn't hear. He needed a hearing aid. They wouldn't give him one. Obviously, he was not the only one who "couldn't hear".

As an MLA, I was inundated with calls from the public. Early on I complained to one of my constituents, who was also an old family friend, that it was difficult for me to "get my work done" due to constant telephone interruptions or from people walking into the office. I was used to working in a law office, where people generally made appointments and didn't call you up unexpectedly.

My friend looked at me. "Eric," he said, "if I were you, I wouldn't worry about people calling all the time. I'd worry if they stopped calling." Later, I saw a saying on someone's office wall to the effect: "I used to resent the interruptions to my job, until I realized that the interruptions *are* my job."

It is true that, as an MLA, your job is to be there, at all reasonable times, for the public. It is they who pay your salary, and they to whom you go at election time for support. As you assume more responsibility in government, you have less time to spend with constituents, and so you must work hard to maintain contact.

As I said, I was relieved I was not in the provincial cabinet for my first term. I wanted to learn the ropes, including the importance of representing all members of the public and listening to them. Of course, listening does not always mean agreeing with everyone. You have to make a decision as to what you feel is in the public interest. Very quickly, some people will say to you that if you do this, or do not do that, they won't vote for you. My reply from early days was always the same: "This is a democracy and it is your prerogative to vote as you feel appropriate, and that is the wonderful thing about a democracy, so do as you please." I think that, ultimately, people respect this approach and support it.

In my first term I already knew that the role of the government MLA involved participating in making difficult choices and defending decisions that are made. Opposition MLAs or MPs simply "oppose". They can be all things to all people, promise anything and agree with every suggestion that comes along, no matter how "hare-brained", or contradictory to the last thing they said.

It was frustrating but humorous to speak to opposition MLAs privately. As both Health minister and Finance minister, individual opposition MLAs would occasionally tell me I was doing the correct things, but would always add, "of course I won't say that publicly." I can remember one vocal Conservative, now a cabinet minister in the Wall government, who would stand up in the legislature and publicly decry conversions of rural hospitals to health clinics that would sit down privately in the legislature and tell me we were "doing the right thing."

One particularly prominent, and vocally negative Saskatchewan Party MLA, now also in cabinet, told me, after I left Finance, that my budgets had been "quite good." But, he said, "We managed to 'trash' every one of them." Such is the nature of opposition.

It is easier to criticize than to create.

The media, too, tends to sell the negative. One day I asked a reporter why they covered the story of the odd person who was not well served by our health care system, but never mentioned the thousands of people successfully treated by the system every day. The response was telling. "Well, Eric, it is not news that the University Bridge is still standing. It will be news if it falls down."

Good news is no news, I guess.

Campaign Managers, Students,
Friends and Dogs (Part 1)

NO MLA WILL LAST VERY LONG WITHOUT an efficient campaign manager, a dedicated network of supporters, and a desire to work collaboratively in an elected role. To establish and keep such a support network operating effectively, the MLA will have to lead by example and often face unseen conflicts that can spring from nowhere. You learn quickly when serving your constituents, doing government business, and canvassing how important your team members and supporters can be.

Occasionally, I have been asked to speak to university, high school or elementary school students about some topic, including the role of the MLA. Invariably, I tell them that the MLA wears many hats. You must be a representative for your constituents in legislative debates and law-making. You must be an advocate for individuals regarding their personal issues, especially if they are being treated unfairly in some way. You must take on committee responsibilities and, if you are appointed to cabinet, you must be responsible to the legislature and the public for the department or agency assigned to you. Thus, you have many public responsibilities, and must juggle your time accordingly.

What is often overlooked, or if it is acknowledged is sometimes disparaged, is that any successful elected politician also has partisan political responsibilities. It is a simple fact of political life that you cannot be elected without organization and money. Canadians should be thankful that federal and provincial governments have limited the amount of money politicians can spend to get elected and also that the public purse subsidizes political campaigns to some considerable extent.

As a result of such management, Canada's elections are much more fair and less money dominated than those of the United States, where no limits exist and where, in reality, only the very rich or those backed by the very rich can be elected. Our system of democracy is better. Still, you need some money, and politicians must keep their political organizations appropriately "peopled" and financed. Otherwise, you cannot win elections, and, therefore, cannot implement any ideas or deliver on your constituents' desired initiatives, however valid.

In fundraising I could always rely upon supporters like Barb Macnab and Ken Rauch to go out and ask members, friends and supporters for contributions. At election time, my wife Pauline joined them. They raised a lot of money. I think they didn't take "no" for an answer. Successful fundraising involves identifying those individuals who are willing to donate, visiting them and asking for money. It is not complicated. Some people give. More do not. You need to identify those with a record of donating, and see them once or twice a year. People give because they are dedicated to the goals of a particular party and want to see the ideals they strongly believe in advanced or, in some cases because they feel a connection to and believe in a particular candidate. Some give wanting a particular advantage, and candidates and parties must be cautious in accepting certain donations. On occasion, where it was accompanied by requests for personal favours, I returned the money.

When I was nominated in 1990, our constituency was already in debt, and about $40,000 had to be raised to retire debt and pay for the 1991 election. In fact, our organization was in the worst financial shape of any constituency in Saskatoon. We resolved to turn things around. We increased our membership, paid off debt and, over the years, put money in the bank. When it came to fundraising, our team was the best.

Politicians also have a financial responsibility to their provincial organizations. I was pleased when our constituency was able to help pay down the debt of the Saskatchewan NDP. In fact one of our constituency members, Ken Rauch, a Commerce grad with his own accounting business, became the provincial party's treasurer in the late 1990s and reduced its debt from over one million dollars to around $600,000. Such management was particularly rewarding for me as I had recruited him to the party, and his efforts were well-appreciated and directly contributed to the election win of 2003. Ken eventually became the president of the provincial New Democratic Party in November 2005.

While it is a fact of political life that you cannot be elected without organization and money, every politician also knows that the vote is always in the hands of the people. When people on the doorstep tell me they don't like politics, or party politics, I ask them whether they believe in democracy. Of course, they always answer, "yes" to which I reply: "How do you have a democracy without politicians and political parties?" Of course, you can't, and everyone who is involved with or contributes to any of our political parties contributes to the democratic process at the same time. It has been my experience that too many take democracy, and all the freedoms we enjoy, for granted.

Each of my election campaigns involved literally hundreds of people — canvassers, telephone canvassers, sign crews, donors, drivers, scrutineers, bakers and providers of food, to name some. Of critical importance are the special roles played by campaign managers, business managers and door-knocking companions, who, like the candidate, are on the front line of campaigning.

In each election, the candidate must have a trusted campaign manager, who really does run the show, especially once the election is officially called. The candidate is not the boss, even if he or she is the premier or a cabinet minister. The campaign manager is the boss, and a smart candidate will do at least two things. First, pick a shrewd and resourceful campaign manager. Second, do what the campaign manager says. That's why you selected him or her. The candidate goes where the campaign manager tells him or her to go. If a particular part of the riding looks questionable, the candidate may be sent there. For example, in the 2003 election my campaign team was upset because the opposition had three or four signs up on a particular crescent, and we had none. This was a real affront to them, because in our campaigns we always "out-signed" the opposition.

So, I was sent out to the crescent and told to knock on all the doors, except, of course, the ones with opposition signs on their lawns. Off I went. As usual, I slowly made my way down the street, since I was chatting and visiting with everyone.

I did manage to get four sign locations, but not at this particular house, where the man inside looked at me and looked at my pamphlet and said he could not vote for me because he didn't want to sell off the crown corporations. "Neither do I!" I said.

"Yes, you do!" he insisted.

"No, I don't!" I countered.

But nothing I could say would dissuade this man from believing I wanted to sell off the crown corporations, so I left. While I was there, I couldn't help but notice that his wife had been laughing at his insistence, and trying to set the man straight, so I hoped that she may have ultimately convinced him to vote NDP. Sometimes, it is hard to say where voters get their information or how they form their opinions. Still, in my experience I have found that the majority of voters are informed. The collective wisdom of the people is valuable, guides a healthy democracy and prevents elites from dominating politics, as the rejection of the Meech Lake Accord demonstrates.

The candidate is also expected to stay out of everyone's way. Your job is to be out there meeting the voters, not pestering everyone at the campaign office. If you ask the campaign manager how many votes they have identified, you won't be told. They don't want pesky candidates bothering them about how they are doing, and they send you on your way.

I made it a point to simply do what they said, and my first campaign manager, Janet Mitchell, called me "the tiny perfect candidate" as a result. By 1995, Janet had relocated and I was in the new constituency of Saskatoon Mount Royal, so I was lucky to inherit Janice MacKinnon's past campaign manager, Barb Macnab. Both managers were highly effective organizers.

Barb was a veteran political activist and a trusted friend. She gave me a lot of good advice and I listened to what she said. By 1999, Barb decided it was time for a new person to learn the ropes and, while she remained active in the riding, we recruited Gayl Basler with the help of Delores Burkart, a local consultant and a strong supporter. It was also Delores who kept me in touch with members of Saskatoon's business community by organizing roundtable discussion groups for me when I was minister of Finance.

Gayl had been an assistant to our former Progressive Conservative MP Ray Hnatyshyn and, after he was defeated in 1988, Gayl worked for PC MP and federal cabinet Minister Jim Edwards from Edmonton. When Gayl joined the team she felt that the provincial NDP government was doing a good job of cleaning up the mess left by the Devine Conservatives, and she wanted to help us out. She was in fact a great help, and managed my campaigns in 1999 and 2003. I also obeyed her.

Candidates each also require a business manager, who must, by law, handle all the money and make sure it is spent legally and that the election spending laws are complied with to the letter. Otherwise, the chief electoral officer, who is now an independent officer of the legislative assembly, hired with the agreement of both sides, can take steps under *The Election Act* to remove you from office, or prosecute you for an offence under the *Act*. Candidates and parties are required to file detailed sworn statements with the chief electoral officer after each election detailing all contributions and expenses. I was very lucky, because "the King" of business managers, Laurence Osachoff, lived in my riding. He knew *The Election Act* inside and out, at least where money was concerned, and was frequently called upon by other business managers for advice. I think Laurence has been a business manager for NDP candidates about fifteen times, four times for me. He also served as the main business manager for all the NDP candidates in Saskatoon, which is a requirement where candidates spend money jointly. Business managers, like campaign managers, have to be obeyed. Needless to say, having someone like Laurence, who had a background in financial auditing, was invaluable. Over the years, Laurence, his wife Tena, and Pauline and I became friends. Tena, Laurence's companion since their teenage years, passed away in December 1996 after many years of marriage. These sad milestones are also shared with people we meet and become close to in public life.

In addition to the guiding diligence of my campaign and political finances, I was also very fortunate to be accompanied by friends and relatives at election time. They came door-to-door, to "leap frog" with me, and we moved through the polls together. It made campaigning more enjoyable, as, at least, if someone swore at you, you could joke around and say, "should I put that one down as undecided?" or some other inane remark. With the right people, campaigning is always fun, especially if those people are family and the kind of friends who know you well.

My sisters, Grace Hansen, Lorea Jantzen and Marg Post have all lent me their support as canvassers from time to time. Voters who get personal can sometimes surprise a candidate's immediate family. On one occasion in 1999, two of them went out together and some enraged voter on her way out of the house looked at my pamphlet and screamed "I WOULD NEVER VOTE FOR HIM!" Unfortunately, this caused my sisters, who can alternate between laughing and crying in sixty seconds, to start laughing hysterically. This was, apparently, not the reaction the voter was expecting, so she jumped in her car, sped away backwards down her driveway, and swerved down the street, narrowly missing several cars. I don't know what I had done to enrage this constituent, but my sisters stood on the street laughing hysterically at this spectacle. I may have lost that vote, but at least they got a good laugh out of it. We went to the bar with several campaign workers afterwards, and they were still laughing. Who says canvassing is always a serious business?

Other family members and friends who have stepped up to help include my cousin Dave Morgan, who canvassed with me in every election. Dave has lived in Star City, Prince Albert, Yorkton, Saskatoon and now Regina, and he seems to know practically everyone in Saskatchewan. He would usually devote a week to each election and tour around the constituency with me. Dave does not like to take "no" for an answer and secured a lot of support for me. One day, however, he decided to take on a Roman Catholic Priest on the abortion question. I had to tell him later that even he couldn't win every argument. Dave's friend, Bob Borreson, also became a friend of mine. He would travel from Alberta to help me out. Bob was another guy who was a natural political candidate. He was always a barrel of laughs, and, in fact, did run for the NDP in Alberta on a few occasions. Obviously, Bob is a courageous man as well as an NDP die-hard.

Another friend, Mel Eldridge, who is a locomotive engineer, could always be counted on to go out campaigning with me as well. Les Gammell, a retired court officer, whom I met when I practiced law, was depended upon for support. Les and his wife Marj, a nurse who only lost by about 400 votes to the Liberals' Lynda Haverstock in the 1995 election, helped me every election. He would campaign for me almost every day, door-to-door, and would often accompany me when I was door-knocking. The dedication of people like Les, who also volunteered for organizations like Cubs and Scouts, is almost breathtaking. Other campaign workers like my neighbour Ruben Peters, who volunteers a lot of time to organizations like the Western Development Museum and the Cancer Society, never cease to impress me. At campaign time a politician needs to be able to count on family and friends. It helps if you always remember that, and keep in touch with people on a regular basis, not just at election time. Politicians forget this at their peril.

While campaigning did prepare me for the kind of personal commitment and friendly support I would need later as a minister of the Crown, it didn't prepare me for how much time I would spend on the road doing government business. Being absent from home a lot, Pauline began to say, without much exaggeration that she often found out where I was or where I was going by listening to the 7:30 AM CBC radio news. Although we spoke by telephone almost every day, we rarely discussed politics or work, so I never told her where I would be the next day, or where I had been. Quite often, wherever I was, the media would ask for some comment on some issue, and I often came back to our home and her in Saskatoon via the radio. Being away from home is a reality for a working politician.

Because I was away a lot, we relied on neighbours to help out. Fortunately for us, our neighbours Lloyd, Sara and Donalyn Schmidt were there attending to things around the house, taking deliveries, clearing snow and the like. As already mentioned, being a politician means that you need a people network, and good neighbours are just as essential as door-knockers.

In so many of my encounters with people, there were those who etched a permanent place in my memory and life. One warm reflection I have is of those in Regina who lent support throughout my incessant travel to the legislature. During my "temporary" twelve-year stay on the second floor of Ken Hodge's house in Regina, Deputy Finance Minister Bill Jones and his family lived on one side of Ken's house and Dick Proctor, MP for Moose Jaw-Palliser, and family lived on the other side.

Ken wasn't much of a drinker and had a dry sense of humour. One day I came home in the middle of the day and Ken, then in his late seventies, was sitting in the living room drinking a beer. As I came in the door he looked up and said, "The deputy minister of Finance lives on one side. The MP lives on the other side. The minister of Finance lives upstairs. Me? I just sit here and drink beer."

What Ken really did, in addition to his legal practice and work as a member of the Law Reform Commission, was to act as a "sounding board" for me and others. Often, when I was perplexed about what to do with a troubling issue, I would come to Ken's place and casually raise the problem. Ken's legal background and life experience usually brought up sound advice, which I usually followed.

Having friends like Ken, and relatives in Regina like my uncle and aunt Ed and Tillie Morgan, as well as cousin Dave Morgan and his wife Linda, meant that there were always people who were willing to hear me discuss personal or political problems. I could speak to them in confidence, at least have someone to listen, get good advice, and often a meal along with it. Valuable, too, were legal colleagues like Murray Hinds for his sound advice, and Angela Bishop for her insight on aboriginal issues.

Without a network of people, no politician can survive. Throughout my political career I have been fortunate to have generous, caring people who have always made a difference whether it was in my years as a backbench MLA, minister or in the early years of campaigning to win a seat.

Of course, every election campaign has its memorable people and stories. Some memories remain for the smallest reasons. Some leave more lasting impressions. One such memory was etched just before the 1999 election. I received a letter from a seventeen-year-old named Joe McMaster. He was coming from the town of Plenty to Saskatoon to enroll in the College of Commerce at the University of Saskatchewan and wanted to get some political experience. I was glad to contact him and asked him to go campaigning with me. Joe came canvassing with me almost every day. The women at the campaign office fondly referred to him as "young Joe". He worked hard and I was pleased and proud to see Joe thrive at his Commerce studies, where he distinguished himself, graduated and went on to work in banking. When you meet young people like Joe, you know there is hope for the future.

Similarly, Brad Bellemare wrote to me wanting to get involved in politics. I worked with him, too, and later encouraged him to consider law school. Years later I received his Master of Laws thesis. It made me proud to see him obtain his Master's degree in law, and I was humbled by an acknowledgment thanking me for playing a role in his success, which was due entirely to his own hard work. Angela Bishop also worked hard on my initial campaigns and went on to earn her law degree while raising her girls. Both Brad and Angela are Métis, and are powerful role models for many others. These are the kind of people memories that remain forever.

Other recollections are equally permanent. One day while canvassing with my neighbour Rick Ewen, I told Rick never to get into an argument with the voters. It never wins votes. Rick and I were out on a crescent in the Westview neighbourhood of Saskatoon and I expect he took my advice to heart, and got along with every potential voter he visited. Unfortunately, after he had finished canvassing, he sat in his truck and listened to me have a somewhat heated exchange at the doorstep of a voter. I think all he could hear was the voter yelling "that's bullshit," and me replying in kind.

The world would certainly be a better place if we could always practice what we preached. But, as I have already said, politicians are human beings too, and I think Rick likely came to the same conclusion.

Another campaign memory I have is of a young student, René Ouellette, who was studying for his Masters in Political Science at the University of Saskatchewan. René was from the francophone part of New Brunswick. After I spoke to some graduate students at the U of S one day, René, who was and is a Liberal, asked me if he could do some political work with me. He wanted to be involved, and felt I would be interesting to work with. He preferred to work for the NDP rather than the provincial Liberals in Saskatchewan, since he saw the NDP as a centrist governing party.

I was happy to oblige. René was full of ideas, strategies and energy. We put him to work organizing a few events, and he also came door-to-door canvassing with me in what we call "between election" canvassing. That is, no election was on, but it is good to get out and talk to the voters. In fact, it is a very good idea, because the voters are always impressed if you don't just show up at election time.

One afternoon in spring 1999, René and I went canvassing in the Massey Place area of Saskatoon. He was going down one side of the street asking people if they wished to see me and I was on the other side. I'm sure René thought that my canvassing must be getting a bit rough when he saw me emerge from a house with blood all over my shirt, holding blood-soaked tissues to my face, and dripping blood onto the sidewalk.

I had been bit in the face by a large German Shepherd dog while talking to the dog's owner in his living room. It all happened very fast, and wasn't the dog's fault. I was sitting in a low armchair petting the dog. I love dogs, and this was a very nice dog named Duke. Anyway, Duke was looking at me, and, if you take note of how you get up out of a low chair, you sort of push your head and shoulders forward rapidly and propel yourself up and out.

Well, my swift move (or not-so-swift as it turned out) startled Duke, whose presence I had forgotten about while talking to his owner. Duke's instant reaction was to bite me in the face. His teeth came through my upper lip completely, so my lip was torn apart. Then, one of his top teeth went into the bottom of my mouth.

The owner and I were both shocked. He gave me a bunch of tissues and hit the dog. I immediately realized what had happened. Duke was standing there looking a bit surprised and confused himself. He was a good dog. I told the owner it wasn't Duke's fault: he was just reacting as dogs naturally do.

Anyway, I thought I should find René and ask him to drive me to the nearby Laurier Drive Walk-In Clinic to get my face sewed up. When we arrived there, the doctor dropped what he was doing to see me, but he said this was a job for the plastic surgeon on emergency call at St. Paul's Hospital and for us to go there immediately.

We went to St Paul's and the surgeon arrived soon and stitched me up. The first doctor had told me if I didn't have it attended to by the plastic surgeon, I would not look the same. Was this good or bad? I wondered. Seriously, I was well cared for and left with only a small scar. This was a political experience I'm sure René will never forget — watching politics and health care in action.

As a result of my encounter with Duke, my face was all puffed up and I had big fat lips, which seemed to go in different directions, especially if I tried to talk. Cynics would say that it was no big deal as most politicians talk out of both sides of their mouths, anyway.

René and I wisely decided not to canvass anymore, although to add to my dilemma, I was scheduled to appear on stage at Persephone Theatre the next day in a fund-raising play.

I knew from a past experience when a feral cat had attacked my face when I was a boy that it was not a good idea to show up at home with unannounced injuries. My mother was quite shocked to see my puffed-up face on that occasion years before. So I reported to Donna Rederburg, my constituency assistant, by telephone, that my face was injured, and would she please track Pauline down and warn her I had had some stitches and my face was swollen. Donna was able to do so, and Pauline was duly prepared before I got home. By the time the play occurred the next night, I looked normal and after we applied some powder over the stitches, I took the stage as planned.

I went back to see Duke a few days later to tell him and his owner all was well. We all had a nice visit, with no quick movements, and the incident was resolved, although it should be noted that the owner's son ran against me in the riding four years later in the 2003 election. The owner had told me in 1999 he was going to vote for me. "I have to, now," he said. Unfortunately, a dog bite is only good for one election and, in 2003, he voted for his son. I'm quite sure Duke would likely have voted for me out of guilt, if he could have. Dogs are very loyal and quite forgiving.

Politicians, Dogs (Part 2) and Other Animals

DUKE WASN'T THE FIRST OR LAST ANIMAL I had a run in with. Earlier in my life when I was staying in Regina, Pauline came down for one of her rare visits to the capital. My former law partner, Doug Kovatch, QC, now a judge, and his wife Shirlene invited us over for supper. We had a nice steak barbeque. When it was time to leave, I escorted Pauline to my two-door 1986 Grand Am, opened the door and she got in. I then opened the driver's side door, and a medium-sized black dog of unknown pedigree bolted up to the car and squeezed behind my bucket seat and sat down in the middle of the back seat.

I moved my bucket seat forward. "Now, come on, doggie, come out of the car," I coached. But, it wouldn't budge. I then approached the dog, but it bared its teeth and emitted a low growl. It wasn't going anywhere.

Pauline became impatient. "Can't you get the dog out? Here, let me try it," which was fine with me. She opened her door, but the dog began to growl and snap at her, and she beat a hasty retreat.

What to do now? I opened both doors and we waited for the dog to leave, but it wouldn't budge. It just sat in the middle of the back seat, looking straight ahead.

After about twenty minutes, I thought I would have to go bother Doug and Shirlene about this dog. It was getting late. Finally I went back to the house and told Doug there was a dog in the car and it wouldn't get out.

"What do you mean there's a dog in the car?" Doug asked.

"Doug, he jumped into the car."

"What do you mean, he won't get out?"

"Doug, he won't get out of the car."

Doug, like Pauline, told me I obviously didn't know how to deal with dogs, so he would get it to move. Out he came, and, after several fruitless attempts, he retreated from the car as well. This dog was a real son-of-a-bitch. Its stubbornness reminded me of some of my caucus colleagues' tenacity when we debated some of my policy initiatives. They could be hard to move sometimes, too. But, at the moment this dog was more committed than any of them.

What to do now? Well, we had had steak for supper so I suggested we take the bones and a few scraps of leftover meat and place them on the sidewalk outside the car. Surely the dog, being a dog, after all, would not be able to resist that. But it did. It just sat there impassively.

I even tried to put some meat in front of the dog, but he wouldn't touch it.

About forty-five minutes passed and I wanted to get some sleep. I suggested that we simply drive to the home of Ken Hodges, QC. (I had moved into Ken's house after being elected in 1991.) In any event, I suggested that we could leave the dog in the car, get some sleep and then drive to the Regina

Humane Society in the morning and let them deal with the damn thing.

"No," Pauline said. She reasoned the dog might eat the upholstery and wreck the interior of the car. At the very least, it might need to relieve itself.

Even though the car was an old one, I thought she was likely right, so we had to come up with another plan. Reluctantly, and feeling sheepish about it, I phoned the Regina City Police and told them a dog had occupied my car and wouldn't leave. They likely thought I was nuts, and I was beginning to wonder myself. "We don't get dogs out of cars. Call the Humane Society," the police service said.

We called the Humane Society, but they had a recording which simply said they were closed, and, in case of emergency, to call the City Police. Well, we'd tried that. Doug, Shirlene, Pauline and I sat around the Kovatch kitchen table for a while strategizing about our next plan of attack. Pauline suggested we should get a blanket and throw it over the dog and pick it up, but we rejected that as too dangerous. What if its head got loose and it bit someone? Doug said he thought he had a large fishing net on a long pole and we could put the net over the dog and pull it out. That sounded like a good plan, but then Doug couldn't find the net.

Finally, I was really tired of this dog's behaviour. Doug and I took a broom and I lunged at the dog with the end of the broom. For a while, it fought and bit the broom but then finally decided to retreat and run out the opposite door.

We never saw the dog again.

The next morning, I was driving in downtown Regina when I saw lawyer Dirk Silversides driving his Jaguar toward me. Since I know Dirk, I stopped my car, rolled down my window, and said hello. He just looked at me. "Have you got a dog in there?" Dirk asked with a smile. I guess word travels fast in a political city like Regina.

As if this ridiculous turn of events wasn't enough, later that same day I drove from Regina to Saskatoon. As I headed north near Aylesbury, I suddenly noticed there was a gopher falling from the sky and it looked like it was going to come through my windshield.

It barely missed the windshield, but landed on the trunk of my car and bounced onto the road. In my rearview mirror, I saw a large bird, a hawk, I think, swoop down and pick up the gopher. I had heard that some birds will kill their prey by dropping them from the sky. I was used to opposition politicians saying the sky was falling, but these intrusions from critters were getting ridiculous.

There were gopher guts on the trunk of my car, but I didn't get around to washing it for a while. It is actually quite hard to get dried gopher guts off of a car, I learned. Had the opposition somehow enlisted the animal kingdom to throw me off my political missions?

Next it was the cat invasion. Dick and Merran Proctor had a cat named Juno. They lived next door to Ken Hodges, where I had been "temporarily" staying for twelve years. One day, Juno decided to climb up to the top of a very tall tree across the street. Cats apparently do climb up trees sometimes and then become afraid to climb down. So, it howled horrifically at the top of this tree. It was there when I went to work in the morning and there when I came home at night. Dick said he called the Fire Department to see if they would come and remove the cat with an aerial ladder, but he had been told that, just as the police don't remove dogs from cars, the Fire Department doesn't remove cats from trees. Dick was apparently also told that there was no reported incident of a cat dying in a tree, and that the cat would eventually come down.

After a few more days of howling, however, somehow the Fire Department relented and came to get Juno. As they approached the cat with the aerial ladder, it jumped down to the roof of the house next door, after which it went into the Proctors' basement and hid for several days. He reminded me of the opposition Conservatives, themselves up a tree, jumping into the Saskatchewan Party, changing their name and hiding from their past.

And there was a further incident. One day I made the mistake of letting a cat into Ken Hodge's house. It looked like Ken's cat but it wasn't. It lived next door with Bill Jones and his wife Marsha Loraas and family. I had already had an experience with a neighbour's cat in Saskatoon moving into our house for short periods and doing damage. Squirrels, obviously trained by the opposition, had moved into our garden shed and eaten my election signs. I knew where this kind of entrance could lead, and I wanted to stop this cat in its tracks.

As unbelievable as this may sound, after the dog refusing to leave my car, this cat started walking around my bed and then parked itself under my bed and decided it would not leave. It also attacked me when I tried to remove it.

I gave up on the cat. I went back to the legislature for the day to fight with the opposition instead. They were kind of mean to me sometimes, but at least they didn't bite or scratch in the physical sense, and most of their actions were predictable.

Meanwhile, I think my animal luck began to improve as I managed to escape an animal episode at home. One of the squirrels in our yard in Saskatoon had fallen down the fireplace chimney and was in our house. I was in Regina, so it was up to Pauline and our good neighbour, Lloyd Schmidt, to deal with it. They did, but I still claim it as another animal encounter that I can add to my list.

Why these animal recollections remain with me through the years is difficult to say. Perhaps it is because the political arena does have its own elements of the wild kingdom. Perhaps it is because these memories remind me that no one has control over all the events in their life. Perhaps these incidents even slightly shape a political will. Whatever the reason, they remain as odd but essential experiences somehow connected to who I am.

Later on in my political life, when opposition member Carl Kwiatkowski wrongly thought that our government was going to require farmers to pay for a licence to shoot intruding coyotes, I immediately took the side of the farmers. Whether or not it was a popular decision, I had had enough of marauding animals and had immediate empathy.

Of course, one thing usually does lead to another. I had been amusing my fellow MLAs with these seemingly non-ending animal stories when I decided to play a practical joke on the rural NDP members. At that time, we had a healthy contingent of farmers in our caucus. Even though both of my grandfathers had been Saskatchewan homesteaders I, of course, grew up in Saskatoon and was a "city boy".

As part of their responsibilities, MLAs often get called to bring "greetings" to meetings and conventions, and someone called to see if I would bring greetings to a meeting of the Game Farmers of Saskatchewan, in my hometown of Saskatoon. It seemed more than fitting and I said I would, but then I thought it would be more appropriate for a farmer to meet them and, perhaps, answer any questions they might have. I asked Walter Jess, MLA for Redberry, if he would attend the meeting instead, and he said he would. The meeting was on a Saturday, and the following Monday when I arrived at the NDP caucus office in Regina, Eric Upshall, MLA for Watrous, and a few other rural members were standing around chatting. One of them asked me how my talk to the game farmers had gone, not knowing that Walter Jess had attended. "Not too well," I said.

They looked concerned. "I misunderstood what I was told," I told them. "I thought it was a meeting of the 'gay' farmers of Saskatchewan."

They looked at me in horror as I continued. "I told them I was not even aware there was an organization of gay farmers, but I congratulated them on forming the organization. At that point, they started yelling at me, and I didn't understand what the problem was."

My colleagues were horrified but I continued to string them along for a while with an increasingly bizarre tale. Eventually, they realized I was pulling their leg, and had a good laugh.

I am sure the plainspoken Walter Jess successfully handled the visit to the Game Farmers of Saskatchewan. Every experience a politician has may become part of political folklore. So it was with some of my animal encounters, which kept my colleagues amused for some time.

Compromise

DURING MY TERM AS A NEWLY ELECTED MLA on the backbenches, I learned that politics involved compromise. While some people believe that you should never compromise your principles, politics always involves compromise. If you are going to do anything at all, you have to make common cause with others. You have to operate as part of a team. Those who are lone wolves do not succeed in politics. They give great speeches and feel very worthy, but they never get anything done. They can't get anything done, because they don't know how to agree on a common agenda with others.

I first learned this valuable principle when I had to do a lot of soul searching over the introduction of Saskatchewan's no-fault insurance in 1994. The scheme was to take effect on January 1, 1995 and would replace the court-based "tort" system that Saskatchewan had up until then.

I was trained as a lawyer that you should never take away the right of people to sue in court for injuries and it went against my grain that in adopting no-fault insurance we were doing so. When I was practicing law, about half of my work involved representing people injured in car accidents, and I had a great deal of sympathy for injured plaintiffs.

At the time I was a member of the Legislative Review Committee, which had to approve the drafting of the legislation. I was also a member of the caucus committee that had to review the legislation and the caucus itself, which ultimately must approve legislation. I was in a position of influence, but I was also in a position of responsibility.

The legislation as originally presented by Saskatchewan Government Insurance (SGI) had what I considered to be many flaws. It gave too much power to the SGI crown corporation to decide what the injured citizen should receive, without much in the way of appeal rights for the citizen. I felt that the injured citizen should have the right to go beyond the insurance company and actually have matters reviewed by a judge in cases where the citizen felt that he or she was being unfairly treated.

I had deep misgivings about the whole idea of no-fault insurance. Nevertheless, the vast majority of cabinet and caucus supported it. Despite their support, I really wondered whether this was something I could endorse. As it happened, the executive of my constituency association was having its monthly meeting during a time when I was most troubled by this issue. It was my habit to run issues by the executive to get their thoughts from time to time, and I took the opportunity to ask what they thought about no-fault insurance.

We had a discussion, during which I was quite surprised at the level of knowledge many of the executive members had about insurance law in general and no-fault insurance in particular. One of the executive members was the son of a judge, and he felt quite strongly that the no-fault system was superior to the court system, even though his father might disagree. Another older member of the executive had a detailed understanding of the original introduction of SGI in the 1940s, which included, originally, a major component of no-fault insurance, which we had drifted away from over the years.

At the end of the discussion, I decided to have a straw vote of the executive to see whether they felt that the government should proceed with no-fault insurance. The vote was twenty-three to two in favour of the government's plan.

I could see that my supporters were asking me to support the plan, and I decided that what I should do would be to work to improve the plan to give more rights to injured people, both in terms of the type of compensation available and their rights of appeal. In fact, I attended hours of meetings where SGI officials were forced to endure what amounted to a tough cross-examination from me about the plan as I made my recommendations.

Many changes were made. For example, the original plan did not permit people to have a judge review whether SGI had properly compensated them. I felt that citizens should have a right of appeal from SGI and that was included. I wanted to avoid a situation where government officials had the power to dictate terms to the injured public. I expected that in all cases they would be well intentioned, and would try to do a good job, but also believed that no one should have too much power over the citizens. As well, originally a widowed spouse did not have the right to claim for lost income his or her spouse might have earned if they had not been killed in a car accident. I felt such a spouse should be able to claim for his or her full economic loss, and appropriate changes were made.

I was pleased, after the legislation was finally prepared, when the senior officials of SGI told me that they felt the no-fault plan was vastly improved as a result of the changes we had made. Consequently, I believe we have the best plan in Canada.

For my part, after the plan was in operation for a few years, I concluded that it was in fact a much better plan than the tort system had been. It clearly provided better coverage, in particular for people who were badly injured and suffered income loss, and I told the officials at SGI that my initial misgivings about the principle of the plan had been wrong.

I learned to play a constructive role to improve legislation that I thought could be improved, rather than simply an obstructive role opposing something I had misgivings about. The whole experience underlined for me the need to work with others to find common cause in order to get things done. I have seen many examples of other MLAs having to make compromises as members of a team and it always works to the betterment of all.

Embarrassment

WHILE AWKWARDNESS AND DISCOMPOSURE are no strangers to politicians who live under the scrutiny of the media and the public, most politicians want to avoid outright humiliation and public embarrassment. There is nothing that can undermine confidence more quickly. Of course, there are large-scale events that happen in the public eye that concern policy and position, where scandal can ruin careers. And then there are the smaller events that just make for momentary worry.

I would advise politicians, other than those who are also elite athletes, to avoid making spectacles of themselves by entering serious foot races or other athletic competitions. Shortly after becoming an MLA, I unwittingly found myself in front of hundreds of spectators competing with some runners who were a lot faster and more fit than I was. I hadn't understood that I was entering a serious race, or that there would be people watching. Yet, I ended up in the race. It was a lot like the dream that many people have where they are in school or somewhere and they suddenly realize they are sitting there in their underwear, or naked. I have had this dream, and my entry into the "Broadway Mile" race in Saskatoon was a similar, but real, experience.

How did this happen? My friend, Saskatoon business-person John Hyshka, knew that I went jogging on a regular basis, usually four or five kilometres per day. He liked to go into 5K and 10K "fun runs" that various groups in Saskatoon sponsored, and insisted that I go along. I had resisted this, but after refusing to go several times, I began to feel guilty about it. My inclination was that I did not want to enter any races, but John was "guilting" me into accepting one of his invitations to go in one of these events.

Finally, one day he got me to agree. He said that there was an event called the Broadway Mile, where hundreds of people run up and down Broadway Avenue in Saskatoon, and no one would even know I was there. Not only that, but, he said, I could enter the "ten-minute mile" category, which would mean I would simply have a slow, leisurely jog up and down the Avenue, along with hundreds of others.

So, we arrived one fall day up on Broadway, and I went to register for the ten-minute mile. Well, there was no such category, but they asked me if I wanted to go in the "eight-minute mile". I agreed. Then it turned out that no one else registered for the eight-minute mile. I was the only one.

My antennae should have gone up and alerted me to the fact that John had given me inaccurate information about the nature of this event, but for some reason that didn't happen, and I blithely agreed with the people at the registration table that they could put me in the "seven-minute mile". For some reason, I still thought that I would be running in the middle of hundreds of people, like pictures of the Boston Marathon I'd seen, and no one would know I was there. I don't know what I was thinking, but the next thing I knew, I was lined up with my fellow runners, across one side of Broadway Avenue.

Now, imagine my shock and horror, when I realized there were only ten of us there. There were about 500 people lined up and down the street, and a man with a gun was about to fire it to start the race. And, these people were serious runners. I wasn't in their league at all. Before I knew it, the gun had gone off, and I realized they were all half a block ahead of me. I couldn't quit the race because I'd have to run through the crowd of spectators and suffer significant embarrassment, so I had no choice. I had to run.

My next mistake, of course, was to panic and run as fast as I could, in a vain and ridiculous attempt to catch up to the others. Before I knew it, they had turned around at the south end of the route and were running in the opposite direction to me.

I had no choice but to keep going and finish the race. As I did so, people in the crowd started yelling things like "way to participate!" Were they being kind, or did they really mean: "why are you in this race?" I didn't know. In any event, the crowd had waited patiently for me to finish the race. I then went off to find John Hyshka, in order to give him a piece of my mind about this "fun run". He was nowhere to be found. I got re-elected in the next election, so I guess it didn't matter that I had lost the "Broadway Mile" so spectacularly and had my moment of embarrassment.

I decided to stick with political races from then on, but was always aware that in the public eye, humiliation can come out of nowhere. While small scale embarrassments like my Broadway Mile run can be seen in retrospect as a humorous moment, large scale events in politics that the media run with are far more dangerous and threatening.

On a few occasions, as a minister, I was presented with information that was embarrassing to the government, usually concerning some screw-up that had occurred. When officials asked me if it should be released, I always asked them to release it, feeling first that the public had a right to know. I also felt that the public and even the media would be more forgiving if we were forthright about what had occurred. They would not tolerate attempts to suppress the truth.

I think a clear example of such a problem occurred in the "Spudco" affair, where the government invested twenty-nine million dollars in money-losing potato barns in the Lucky Lake area. It was not just the loss of money, but the fact that government representatives misled the public by portraying it as a "public-private" investment when it was all government money. If the government had simply said it was building public or cooperative potato barns for twenty-nine million dollars, no one would have batted an eye. It would have been seen as a good investment in valuable infrastructure, which potato barns certainly are.

The attempt to dress up a project that could have been done in a straightforward way as something that it was not ultimately led to a great deal of distrust, allegation and embarrassment for those identified by the media and the public to be responsible.

When it comes to the public's business and money, honesty really is always the best policy.

Minister of the Crown and the Civil Service

I WAS ELECTED FOR MY SECOND TERM in June 1995. In November, Premier Romanow phoned me at my constituency office in Saskatoon and asked me if I would join his cabinet. I said I would be honoured to do so.

Naturally, I wondered what portfolio he had in mind, but I didn't ask. He said that he saw me as either minister of Justice or minister of Labour, and asked me to come to Regina to meet him at 5:00 PM, two days later. I felt that either of these portfolios would be suitable for me, since I was a lawyer, and had practiced some labour law, both in court and before arbitration panels.

After two days, at the appointed time, I went to Roy's office. After being escorted in, we sat opposite one another. I wondered what this new role would bring, but felt that, for sure, my life was about to change and become more complex. I didn't fully appreciate what the new demands might be like until Roy spoke. "I have decided that tomorrow morning you will be sworn in as minister of Health. This will either make you or break you," he said.

I was shocked and surprised. I knew that the health portfolio was one of the toughest, especially at that time, when we were in the throes of health reform. My immediate reaction was that he was throwing me into the deep end and seeing if I could swim. Health reform had been ably begun by Louise Simard, who had not contested the 1995 election, having returned to the private practice of law. Louise is a smart and gutsy person, who did a great job. But, the public had not fully accepted the need for change in our health care system. Change had to continue, but in a manner and at a pace with which people could cope.

I was naturally aware of the controversy surrounding health reform, and of the fact that, since 1993, two ministers, Simard and Lorne Calvert, had been handling the health portfolio. The conversion of fifty hospitals to health centres had created wounds in rural Saskatchewan, which had not yet healed, since the range of services made available at health centres had not yet become widely understood. The decision to encourage seniors to remain in their own homes with appropriate supports like home care, as an alternative to institutionalization, was viewed by some as cold and heartless rather than an advance in quality of life, which it truly is.

Clearly, I would have my hands full, but I wasn't about to turn the offer down, since I welcomed the challenge, wanted to serve, and basically just didn't know any better.

Breaking the news to Pauline and a few of my legislative colleagues, including Biggar MLA Grant Whitmore, I realized this came as a big surprise to people close to political circles. The media was also taken by surprise, given my status as a rookie minister and my lack of health care expertise. Normally, new ministers are assigned junior portfolios. But, no one was as surprised as I was to find myself in charge of this, the biggest and most costly, portfolio of government.

When you become a minister of the Crown, you are presented with "briefing books". These are prepared by the civil service, and contain every conceivable issue that might arise. In the case of the Department of Health, they are at least one foot thick, crammed with minute detail about everything from the number of people waiting for cataract removal to the salaries of doctors and specialists. No time, however, is allocated to reading these before one's duties as minister begin. First, there is the swearing in at Government House, followed by the first of many media "scrums" (which I came to privately call "feeding frenzies") where the media took to stirring the pot that is health care politics. My first scrum was right after the swearing in at Government House, ten minutes after I became minister.

So, there I was, the newly-minted minister, much to everyone's surprise, and the first question put to me was — "What is your stand on abortion?" I hadn't anticipated the question. I instinctively knew that what the media wants is a story. They want me to say, "I don't know," so they can write a headline which says, "Minister unsure what abortion policy should be". Or, they might want me to say, "I am personally opposed." Then, the headline would be "Health minister opposes NDP policy on abortion".

At least I knew that the government had a policy. I knew what the policy was and that it was my job as a minister to enunciate government policy. I also knew that if you can't support the policy of your government, you shouldn't be a cabinet minister. I was ready for them. "It is the policy of our government that abortion is a matter of choice to be decided between a woman and her physician, and I support the policy of the government," I said.

I guess this answer did not leave much room for follow-up questions. The reporters looked at me. I looked at the reporters. No story there. It was the only question during that first media scrum in which there was a potential trap concerning personal beliefs. I had survived this first feeding frenzy.

That same day, I hit the road running. Within twenty-four hours, I was off to public events in Saskatoon, Birch Hills and Smeaton. Questions from the media about health policy were asked and I answered them. Briefing notes for every event were provided by competent civil servants from the Department of Health, dedicated people whose contribution to the public good and welfare is often overlooked, but on whom I depended in those first few weeks and beyond.

Of course not every civil servant in the department was equally helpful or supportive. Early lessons from civil servants in the Department of Health surprised me about what officials sometimes expected from their elected leaders. Some in the Department of Health, although led by the competent and respected Duane Adams, had strange ideas about the role of the minister. Duane himself was a very responsive and veteran public servant, who unfortunately passed away a few years later. But while there were those like Duane who understood collaboration, there were others who were less accommodating.

One example of civil servant discord became known from comments made to me by a lawyer friend from Prince Albert. He told me that he had asked an official in the Department of Health, who was also a friend of his, how I was doing as minister of Health. "Okay," she replied, "but we have some problems with his ethics."

My friend, who was also a former legal associate, expressed surprise, saying he felt I was regarded as an ethical professional. "What do you mean?" he asked.

The reply startled him. "Well, he doesn't always do what we say." My friend found this quite amusing. "He's the minister," he pointed out. "He doesn't have to do what you say." This reality was lost on some parts of the health bureaucracy, which, in some ways, seemed to be a law unto itself. The size of the health department, which prior to health reform devolution to the local districts, was a huge department, probably contributed to the attitude, held by some within it, that the department was a government unto itself. They had a lot of weight to throw around, and some seemed to consider their power as greater than that of an elected department minister.

When he asked me to take on the job, Roy Romanow also said he wanted me to "take control" of the department. I may not have fully understood what he meant at that moment, but by the time I was moved out of there twenty months later, I sensed that my efforts to "take control" had not been appreciated in all quarters. I knew that bureaucrats in health and some of the heath districts had complained to the premier about what they considered my overbearing ways. On a few occasions, Roy called me up on the carpet, having heard one side of a particular story. When I explained the other side, he cooled down and assessed the situation fairly. On one occasion, for example, one of the health board chairs went to see Roy and told him I was being "high-handed" and ordering them around. When I explained that the man had phoned me to ask me if I was "serious" about my comments on the radio that health districts should operate within set budgets, Roy's views changed. I had, indeed, told the gentleman that budgets actually were intended to be followed. That was my job as an elected representative and appointed minister.

A pertinent example of this inability of some to respect the elected representative of the people concerned an information campaign the Department of Health proposed shortly after I became minister. Every three years the health cards given to every Saskatchewan resident over eighteen years of age expire and must be renewed. Because many people move, get married, or change their name in three years, the department must update its records to ensure renewal stickers get sent out to everyone.

The department sent me a package that contained the publicity campaign they intended to use to reach the households of Saskatchewan. Part of it was a brochure that said on the front page: "Your health care coverage will end on December 31".

This was intended to get everyone's attention, and get them to take seriously the need to let the department know their current address and other vital information.

We were in the midst of a situation across the province where people were very upset with a lot of health care changes going on. I felt that people, particularly the elderly, could misunderstand and be upset by the brochure, and think their cherished health coverage was now being taken away. There was so much talk in the news of a health care "crisis" that the chance that people could misunderstand the intent of the brochure was significant. As health minister I knew that we didn't need to upset people any more than they may already be. We didn't need the hassle ourselves. We had enough trouble already.

I instructed my office staff to inform the department that this brochure was not to be sent out. Another version was needed to address the potential miscommunication. The response of the communications branch of the department was revealing. *"We did not send that to him for his approval. We sent it to him for his information."* In other words, they actually felt they should simply be able to tell me what they were doing and just do it. I was to have no opinion on it, let alone express that opinion. I was flabbergasted and, perhaps for one of the few times in my life, speechless. But I collected myself, and succeeded in getting the brochure changed before it went out. Bear in mind that this directed change in the brochure was considered, by some, to be "unethical behaviour" on my part. How it could be misconstrued as such remains a mystery to me to this day.

One other more amusing anecdote of my time as minister of Health comes to mind. When I became the minister in 1995, I was quite shocked to be signing letters to members of the public who had written the previous minister a year earlier. I told my staff to inform the department that the public was entitled to an answer within a few weeks and, if the letter could not be fully answered, it had at least to be acknowledged within that time, with a full response to follow.

After some months, one of the communications people in the department informed Murray Gross, an able ministerial assistant in my office, that they "did not have time to meet the minister's deadlines," they "had other things to do" and we would have to accept that timely responses to the public were not practical. Murray's duties included ensuring letters were answered in a reasonable fashion, and he brought the department concern to my attention.

I thought I had already heard it all, but apparently not. When Murray told me this, I phoned Mark Seland, the director of Communications in the department. I told Mark that his subordinate had some very interesting ideas that had been expressed to Murray Gross. I repeated my views about the right of the public to receive timely responses. I said, however, that I was intrigued by the views expressed by the department official, and I wanted that official and Mark to come to my office to discuss these views with me personally.

As I fully expected, the meeting to discuss the views was never arranged. Most importantly, they decided they had the time, after all, to get around to answering the public's letters. So I had won that battle. Why, however, would you have to have a battle over something like that in the first place?

I have never tired of relating these stories. Even now, I am between amusement and disbelief. Could such bureaucratic nearsightedness as this really happen to an elected minister of the Crown? Well, it did.

Part of my run-ins with health officials probably arose from the fact that I listened carefully to the elected MLAs and tried to make the system more sensitive to their views and those of their constituents. If the civil service feels they should have a monopoly on making all decisions, with no input from elected people (which some of them invariably felt was political interference) shouldn't they have to get elected themselves? Certainly they did not have the monopoly on all the good ideas or what was best for Saskatchewan voters. Many of their ideas were, in fact, unpopular with the public. For example, during the health care reforms they wanted to convert yet more hospitals to health centres. But, the pace of change in terms of health care facilities was not always workable, and the civil service didn't really understand that. They were in their offices, not talking to people on the ground. Many of the Saskatchewan people who witnessed the rapid health care facility changes became alarmed and often felt insecure because they thought the designation "hospital" meant they would be taken care of in the event of emergency and "health centre" implied that they wouldn't be. Dialogue was needed, and people needed to know what the changes meant. To suggest yet more change, at that point, complicated the problem.

There was, however, significant work accomplished during my first ministerial appointment. The major issue for me as Health minister, of course, was the model of health reform, which continued to be implemented. It had been conceived by the Department of Health under the able leadership of Louise Simard and Duane Adams, with the full support of Premier Romanow, the cabinet and virtually the entire caucus, with the notable exception of Glen McPherson, then MLA for Shaunavon, who departed for the Liberals. Louise was a competent and courageous minister of Health, and Duane Adams was no slouch either.

There is no question in my mind, and now I think in just about everyone's mind, that Louise Simard's model of health reform was needed and correct. As difficult as it was to introduce such radical reform, the fact is that Saskatchewan had 125 hospitals for a million people. That was as many as Ontario had for eleven million. More importantly, the services these hospitals could provide often were not what the population needed.

What was the point of staffing operating rooms in hospitals where there were no surgeons, no anaesthetists and, in one case, no babies born for eighteen years? Why not convert these "non-hospitals" in reality to health centres that would actually provide needed services to people in small-town Saskatchewan?

While Louise was criticized for "closing fifty-two hospitals" in fact she didn't. Fifty-one were converted into health centres and one ultimately became an eating disorder recovery centre.

From 1995 to 1997, the controversy and trumped-up "health care crisis" went on and on. Many of the fears and much media coverage was generated by the vested interests of those who simply did not wish change to occur because it interfered with their jobs, positions, or ways of doing things. It was a highly political, often self-interest laden grievance in which the public was left to wonder whom to believe. Was their health and well being jeopardized? No, but it made for sensational media coverage and provided plenty of fodder for the opposition to grill the minister of Health in question period.

So it was that, as a rookie minister, I entered the legislative session in the spring of 1996. No one could have adequately prepared me for the barrage of questions that came in that session. It was very difficult for me. I was under unending attack from the opposition and parts of the media. The record shows that I was in the hot seat far more than anyone else the entire session. It was baptism by fire. I guess Roy was right that the job would "make me or break me." I think it almost broke me.

I did the best I could do. My approach was to "fight fire with fire" and to give as good as I got. As the opposition attacked the government, through me, each day in question period, I attacked them back with vehemence.

Of course, the opposition must do its job and ask ministers lots of questions. Often, their allegations in question period are intentionally a bit "over the top." The nature and tone of their questions is to push for reaction and you often feel like you're answering a question like, "Have you stopped beating your wife yet?"

So, for example, as Hansard, the legislative verbatim transcript, records, the never very subtle Bill Boyd, then Progressive Conservative MLA for Kindersley asked whether "your plan to destroy rural health care is completed?" (April 10, 1996) Of course, in the meantime, Glen McPherson couldn't resist alarming health care workers who allegedly would "not be receiving their regular pay cheque tomorrow because the South Central Health District has insufficient funds with which to pay them," (April 11, 1996). That would be a first, of course. But, then, according to Glen, "our health care system is an inferno here in Saskatchewan . . . ", and in "chaos," (April 17, 1996).

If you listened to then Liberal MLA Rod Gantefoer from Melfort, however, I was probably too busy to notice, since I was fully occupied attacking seniors:

> The minister doesn't have the guts to come to Melfort to do it himself, his own dirty work, and tell the seniors that he is throwing them out of their homes that he's going to do it personally. (May 7, 1996)

His colleague Glen McPherson did not want to be outdone and wanted to strike his own blow "You've kicked people out of nursing homes," he alleged, and "our sick and elderly are terrified of your health care system," (May 9, 1996). And who wouldn't be terrified listening to them? Then Humboldt Liberal MLA Arlene Jule disagreed with them slightly. She felt the seniors were not "terrified", but "frantic". She also alleged that I was going to cut nursing home beds and throw a one-hundred-year-old woman who had had her leg amputated out onto the street. "Now she and her family are wrought with worry about what will happen to her if nursing home beds are cut," she said. (May 9, 1996).

It was my job to answer these allegations. Calm and rational answers are not as newsworthy as wild allegations, but you just have to try.

So I gave Ms. Jule and the legislature an answer that was quite typical of what I needed to say to them:

Mr. Speaker, it saddens me that members of the legislature would get up and suggest that elderly people in nursing homes would be taken out of their homes and would have no place to go, and that that has happened or that it would happen because, Mr. Speaker, it has not happened, even though those members continue to say that it has happened. And, Mr. Speaker, it will not happen. Mr. Speaker, this is simply alarmist fear mongering from the Liberals. They have been at it for a long time. (May 9, 1996).

My reference to their history of fear mongering goes back, of course, to the proud record of the Saskatchewan Liberal Party when Medicare was introduced into Saskatchewan in the early 1960s. It galled me that these people, who along with their Conservative friends went to any length to stop Medicare, including the ruining of careers and reputations and frightening the dickens out of anyone prepared to listen to them, were now the great defenders of public health care. But voters, of course, often have a short memory.

The nurses got into the act, too. They provided the opposition with horror stories every time a doctor or nurse did something wrong. According to then Saskatchewan Union of Nurses President, later NDP MLA Judy Junor, this showed "we've got a health care system in crisis," (quoted by Melville

Liberal MLA Ron Osika, May 19, 1996). The nurses are still at it today. The health care system, according to them, has now been "in crisis" for over thirteen years.

What bothers me most about this type of rhetoric is the lack of appreciation of what we, in Canada, enjoy, compared to the rest of the world. Canadians do not live in "crisis". We have problems, for sure. We can do better for sure. But in most parts of the world, there is no health care system for ordinary people. If they get sick, often they just die. Not to mention that people in other parts of the world often don't even have clean water or a roof over their heads, compounding their health conditions. On the political stage we often seem incapable of acknowledging our good fortunes.

One day the media were questioning me in a scrum. One of them asked about the "health care crisis". I said, "Canadians do not live in crisis. People in Bosnia and Rwanda live in crisis. We do not. We have problems to deal with." They may have thought I was simply in denial, or that I was being "arrogant", since they loved to accuse me of that if I dared to disagree with the premise of their questions. In fact, the language in the question offended me, given how privileged we are in this country.

But, of course, it is the language in question period that gives it its colour. According to Rod Gantefoer from Melfort, long-term care was "callous and inhumane", leading to "the sick and the elderly" being "subjected to a great deal of stress and anxiety as they are left to fend for themselves . . . Eighty-seven-year-old Minnie Woods says of this government's action, and I quote: 'It's brutal, it's cruel . . . they're turning us out on the street' . . . "

But Rod needed to up the ante even more, quoting another resident, who asked: "Why not just say you have to die at age 65?" (May 21, 1996).

Good grief! Thank God my parents weren't alive to see me presiding over this callous, inhumane, brutal, cruel, terrifying system! What could I say to confront such numbing accusations?

> It is not helpful to the situation of people who may be feeling some anxiety as a result of the change, Mr. Speaker, to have people suggesting that they will be thrown out on the streets or that they will not have a home. It is true that some people, Mr. Speaker, will be going from one home to another, but I assure the member and I assure the House that these people will have a good home and a decent home, Mr. Speaker. (May 21, 1996)

Nevertheless, Rod Gantefoer continued: "Government forces seniors from their homes," (May 21, 1996). Then Conservative MLA Don Toth insisted that government was "throwing (them) out of their homes," as part of "a pretty heartless and gutless plan," and "a heartless blow," (May 22, 1996).

But there was still more to endure: "Government is directing its venom at the most defenceless in our society, the severely disabled . . . " (Liberal Harvey McLane, June 4, 1996) as part of an "inhumane system in which people have to die before others can receive proper care," (former Liberal Saltcoats MLA Bob Bjornerud, June 14, 1996). This was probably just part of our "long-term plan to decimate rural Saskatchewan," (former Liberal MLA June Draude, June 18, 1996).

Later, of course, I moved to Finance, where I could be accused of all kinds of financial mismanagement and chicanery, and Industry and Resources where the opposition once described Saskatchewan's booming 2006 economy as in "a death spiral". In 2007, the opposition referred to the (still booming) Saskatchewan economy as suffering from "Lorne Calvert's reign of economic terror". I guess a lot of people must have believed them, since they formed government later that year.

In retrospect, notwithstanding almost daily provocations, I know now that I responded too aggressively on occasion. On the other hand, the opposition was out to get us. It is their job. And, when you truly believe you are making changes that ultimately are in the public interest, you must defend that principle. I did so, but when the 1996 legislative session came to an end, no one was more relieved than I was. The last day of the 1996 spring legislative session, I was physically and emotionally exhausted.

As a result of my baptism by fire, I quickly developed a reputation as a scrappy debater in question period, and discovered that there actually is an audience of some thousands that watches question period every day. The office would get phone calls and emails after a particularly hot time in question period. Most of these were from supporters who would take the time to send a message that they liked the job I had done. Undoubtedly, there were a lot of people watching who didn't like what I had to say as well. However, a small and dedicated cheering section urged me on. One of my biggest question period fans was my brother Don who, along with my friend Don Zolmer, insisted on being provided with a tape of question period after each session. My brother would have a great time watching question period and developed a real disdain for the Liberal, Conservative and Saskatchewan Party members who went after me. If you can't count on your brother to support you, you're in trouble. Through these sessions in question period I honed the debating skills that I would need during the rest of my political journey.

As Health minister, I tried to move the health reform file along. I piloted *The Health Facilities Licencing Act* through the House to promote, protect and preserve public Medicare, something in which I believe very passionately. The *Act* outlawed facilities from providing insured health services unless licensed by government. The legislation ensured that access to health services must be based on need, not the ability to pay. This is a basic principle of Medicare, and is very important.

Health care politics is, in fact, what led me to become interested in, join and represent the New Democratic Party in the first place. The Cline family, which settled in and around Zelma, Saskatchewan, had always been strongly Liberal. My great-grandfather, his wife and eight adult sons and five daughters came to Saskatchewan more than a century ago. They took out nine homesteads, one of which was my grandfather John Cline's homestead. He and my mother's father John Morgan, a homesteader who became an implement dealer in nearby Colonsay, were both active Liberals.

In the early 1960s, the Saskatchewan CCF-NDP government brought Medicare to Saskatchewan. This had been a longstanding policy of the party. I was only seven years old when Premier Woodrow Lloyd oversaw this development, and, of course, it escaped my attention. But for some reason, by the time I was twelve, I started following this issue. I knew that the principle of Medicare was that if someone was sick, we should care for that person together. I understood that the NDP, as it became known, had stood for this principle. I believed that the Liberal party had defeated the NDP in 1964 over this idea. I felt that the Liberals were wrong about this. In a very simple way, I decided that the idea of Medicare was correct and that if the NDP was behind this idea, then I was a supporter of the NDP. Although my dad had "ordered" my older sister to vote Liberal in the 1967 provincial election — "This household is Liberal and as long as you live under my roof you vote Liberal" — by 1968 they, along with most of the province, were too angry with Premier Ross Thatcher's government to worry about my developing political ideas.

Given the long history of Medicare, I should have known the Health portfolio would be difficult. And as soon as I was assigned the portfolio, I should have been more attentive to a conversation I had with Lorne Calvert, the departing minister of Health, on the day of my swearing in to cabinet.

Lorne was becoming minister of Social Services the same day. I was being assigned the office he had occupied, and Louise Simard before him. I told Lorne it was not necessary for him to move, that I could take another office. He told me that this was not possible. He said that that particular office had to be the office of the minister of Health because the safe outside it contained "important health related information and documents."

I took his word for it and didn't give it any more thought. A few weeks into the job, however, I asked my secretary, Shirley Richardson, what was in that safe. "Christmas decorations, and some of Louise Simard's old junk," Shirley said. I realized at that moment that Lorne had been in a hurry to get out of that office. I also should have suspected the reason.

During my time as Health minister, I did have supporters in the Department of Health and many health districts. People who felt I was trying to listen and combine the need for health reform with some sensitivity to local concerns appreciated my efforts. These supporters, however, did not win the day. I think complaints about my on-going debates with health care officials in the department and the districts was one factor in the decision to move me out of Health, although I also think Premier Romanow wanted to move a new person into Finance, which is eventually where I went. In retrospect maybe that explains why there were two ministers managing the Health portfolio before it was handed to me: one to get things done and another to meet with the health officials network.

I was moved from Health to Finance in a major cabinet shuffle in late June 1997. I later learned from Department of Finance officials that a senior health official phoned to warn them about me. When that Health official was told that, so far, they had really enjoyed working with me, they were warned, "Well, wait for the other shoe to drop." In fact, I got on famously with the Department of Finance from top to bottom. I enjoyed working with them, and by all accounts, they enjoyed working with me. They were thoroughly professional and seemed to have no problem with the notion that a cabinet minister might actually have ideas and might express them from time to time. But, I do not wish to leave the impression that I do not respect or value the public servants in the Department of Health. In fact, I do respect the vast majority of them. They were going through a difficult time, under scrutiny for making sweeping health changes. Some, however, simply did not appreciate the two-way relationship that should exist between minister and department.

The Inside Staff

NO MINISTER OF THE CROWN HAS EVER SUCCEEDED without the usually invisible and unacknowledged help from ministerial secretaries and assistants — the inside staff.

Walking into the health ministry was no easy task. But, arriving with me were a very seasoned veteran ministerial secretary, Shirley Richardson and her colleague from Bob Pringle's office, Gloria Kups. These two were godsends.

As I sat at home in Saskatoon the weekend after my swearing in reading the briefing books, Shirley and Gloria were setting up shop in our legislative building office. They had previously worked for Bob Pringle, MLA for Saskatoon-Eastview, who had voluntarily left cabinet as I was going in.

Shirley had been a minister's secretary for many years, with the notable exception of the Devine years when, as a divorced mother trying to raise two children, she was fired at the instigation of a Conservative minister. Of course, she was just one of hundreds of Saskatchewan citizens sacrificed on the altar of politics during that era. Gloria was more newly minted, and Shirley became the senior secretary.

The principal role of the senior secretary is to organize the minister's life. In a minister's work life there is too much to do, too many people to see, and too little time. Your secretaries have to keep it all moving. It isn't easy, because the schedule is a moving target. Just when they get you organized, the premier calls a special cabinet meeting, or the prime minister calls for a health summit, or whatever. The secretaries manage it all.

Shirley, now retired, was one no-nonsense person. I liked her a lot, but I knew better than to disagree with her. We had had a disagreement once, and both of us decided we were too headstrong to clash again. Gloria went on to become a senior ministerial secretary in another office and Shirley eventually retired, having groomed her successor, Lynette Herauf, a young farm wife who was very competent, but, unlike Shirley, quite quiet. While Shirley's plain-spoken manner was usually very effective in getting the job done, there was one occasion when her frankness went a bit too far.

Various groups come to visit the cabinet throughout the year and present their views. This occurs on what they call "Cabinet Delegation Day". One day, the Saskatchewan Francophone organization came to visit. The Francophones were duly assembled on one side of the NDP caucus room and the cabinet sat across at tables on the other side. While presenting their brief, the president indicated that while Francophones were entitled to service from their government in French, this was not always recognized. For example, she said, they had written to a cabinet minister in French, and the minister's secretary had called them demanding that the letter be sent again, in English. When they explained that they felt it was their right to communicate in French, they had been told clearly that their letter would not be dealt with unless it was received in English.

Ironically, during the discussion part of the meeting, I indicated to the group that I was very disappointed to hear what they had to say about that incident, and assured them that this was not the policy of the government. After the meeting, the president of the group came up to me. "Mr. Cline," she said, "we did not wish to embarrass you, but the office we were talking about was your office."

Of course, I apologized profusely, and went back to my office to discuss the matter with my chief of staff, Duane Haave. I told Duane what had happened, but he already knew about it. He said that Shirley had come to see him sometime before. "I think I may have done something wrong," Shirley had said to him. She had taken it upon herself to raise her *faux pas* with Duane. They had discussed the fact that there is a translation service available to government, and they had proceeded to correct the situation. I was relieved that the matter had been dealt with, but also had to smile at Shirley's recognition that the days of making light of the constitutional right of francophones to communicate with their government in French were over.

I raise this as one of the incidents that happen in politics that you can look back on with some humour. At the time, of course, it was a little more serious as there was a problem that had to be solved. I do not mean to leave the impression that Shirley was other than a very kind and competent person. Shirley was a wonderful secretary but, like everyone else, including me, she wasn't right one hundred percent of the time.

As a new minister, I relied heavily on Shirley not only to organize my schedule but also to advise me on the protocol of being a minister. On the day Shirley retired, Judy Samuelson, Roy Romanow's chief of staff, was trying to get me to agree to a policy that I did not want to agree to. She was using all kinds of arguments to get me to see things her way, but I wouldn't budge. Finally she used what I suppose was her trump card. "Well," she said, "the premier wants you to do this."

I didn't believe that the premier really cared about the issue but, in any event, I still didn't budge. "Judy," I said "there is only one person in this building that could order me to do this, and she's retiring today."

I was sorry to see Shirley retire, but I was glad she would have more time to spend with her partner Cal, children, grandchildren and her beloved garden. At her retirement party in our office, I gained a valuable insight into the respect she commanded. Shirley had worked for Norman Vickar when he was a minister in Allan Blakeney's government before 1982. Mr. Vickar now lived in Winnipeg, but he and Mrs. Vickar had taken the time to drive to Regina and were standing in my office at the retirement party. I told Mr. and Mrs. Vickar that I thought it was very nice and thoughtful of them to come all the way from Winnipeg for Shirley's party. Mr. Vickar then related a story to me. Before his election as the MLA for Melfort in the 1970s, he had been a respected businessman there. After his defeat, a new government building in Melfort was named in his honour. Shirley and other former members of his staff had travelled to Melfort to attend the ceremony. Mr. Vickar had spoken at the ceremony, but afterwards realized he had forgotten to acknowledge and thank his legislative staff. This had bothered him all these years, and now it was almost twenty years later.

At the time the staff hadn't even noticed, or felt slighted at all. But here he was, making sure that he came to Shirley's retirement and, after I asked him if he would like to say a few words, he took the opportunity to acknowledge her service and publicly express his appreciation to his staff and his regret that he had not acknowledged them so many years before.

Sometimes, little things make a very lasting impression. I already had a high opinion of Norman Vickar, but I felt that I gained further insight into his character on that day.

I demand hard work, excellence and public service, from persons working for me. I am hard on myself, and others, when we fail to measure up. I try to acknowledge good work and my staff knows that I appreciate them. I am very fortunate to have worked with excellent people over the years including secretaries like Shirley, Gloria, Angie Berjian, Jacquie Mann, Colleen Campbell, Crystal Smith and Lynette along with long time chief of staff Duane Haave and able ministerial assistants including Murray Gross, Tyler Lloyd, Brian Humphreys, Donna Fincati, Sherry Miller, Kim Newsham, Michelle Oussoren, Heath Packman, Catherine Yates, and David Froh. Recognizing these people is important, for it is always the collaboration of skilled people who make the difference in political work and the "inside" staff is essential to this process.

Managing the Province's Finances

IN JUNE 1997, PREMIER ROMANOW ASKED ME to move from Health, and to become minister of Finance. Once again, until the day before the cabinet shuffle, I was unsure what my new duties would be, but it is always the premier's prerogative to pick his cabinet. He had said that he was going to move me either to Justice or Finance despite the fact that one of my colleagues was lobbying very hard to become the new finance minister. Premier Romanow had other plans. And though my colleague was unsuccessful in his lobby, he remained on Treasury Board. Such political friction is often present in a cabinet shuffle.

So there I was, the new minister of Finance and chair of the Treasury Board. I had never been on Treasury Board, and did not know its procedures. My vice-chair was Janice MacKinnon, who had served as Finance minister for the past four years. It was quite an adventure to chair the Treasury Board with a strong-willed former Finance minister as vice-chair and another member who had wanted my job. But, it was my job to act as chair and, as in all my political appointments, I accepted the responsibility, persevered, and went on to present five provincial budgets. My appointment as minister of Finance would prove to be the longest tenure at Saskatchewan Finance since Clarence Fines stepped down from the job in 1960.

One of the interesting aspects of serving as minister of Finance is meeting the federal, provincial and territorial counterparts once or twice per year. They tend to be very senior and able members of their governments, and it is a pleasure to meet them. Since Paul Martin was the federal Finance minister for almost all of the time I held the portfolio in Saskatchewan, I saw him at least a few times per year, spoke to him occasionally by telephone, and got to know him pretty well. He was a very accomplished businessperson, blunt and able, and a very competent Finance minister. You knew where you stood with him, what he was willing to do, and what he would not do. I appreciated his straightforward approach. On a personal level, he was a very modest and personable individual, and I always enjoyed talking to him. I think he served Canada very well as Finance minister in the 1990's, bringing in some very progressive policies like support for innovation and, of course, most importantly, balancing the federal budget. His fiscal prudence has served Canada very well, and set our country on a new financial footing.

In all discourse and debate Paul Martin was, as I said, a straight shooter. But, his approach seemed to change once he became prime minister. Paul Martin's decency and smarts were not enough to keep him focused once he finally achieved his dream of being prime minister. Like many other politicians who rise in power, the demands of leadership resulted in what was at least a perceived lack of any coherent national agenda. His place in history will likely be remembered for that as much as his financial prowess.

While these federal-provincial-territorial meetings are part of the responsibility of ministers of the Crown to share ideas and co-ordinate national planning, a definite fringe benefit is that you meet with your counterparts from across the country, and get the opportunity to encounter many interesting and colourful characters.

Both Premiers Romanow and Calvert were strong advocates for Saskatchewan. Both, as well, are proud Canadians. The tone they expected their ministers to adopt in dealing with other governments was to strongly advocate for Saskatchewan's interests, but also to also try to co-operate and seek consensus among the federal government, other provinces and territories. This was never easy, since there are many voices around the table, with widely differing views, some louder than others.

It soon become apparent that Alberta and Ontario could always be counted on to strut around telling everyone else how things should be done. Alberta's Stockwell Day and Ontario's Ernie Eves were aggressive personalities. Listening to Stockwell Day tell us all how to do things, I realized that just about anyone could handle the finances of Alberta, Canada's richest province. I couldn't believe that the Canadian Alliance elected him to lead them in opposition in Ottawa, and was not surprised when he eventually rode off on his jet-ski into the sunset. On the day that he was elected leader, I gave my prediction to my colleagues: "This will not work," I said. In fairness to Mr. Day, however, he went on to serve ably as a minister in Stephen Harper's Conservative government; tenacious people will often emerge successfully after a disaster that would stop others.

Ernie Eves was a very capable Ontario minister who on some occasions had a quick wit and a way with words. At one meeting I remember him accusing federal Finance minister Paul Martin of "throwing nickels around like they were manhole covers." I thought that this was a colourful and, at the time, apt comment. Of course, Paul Martin did start throwing big money around quite liberally several years later when he became prime minister and was trying to hold on to power.

If Alberta and Ontario could be counted on to try to set the agenda for the rest of us, Quebec could always be counted on to promote its own nationalist agenda. BC was, well, BC. They were predictably unpredictable. So, it was always up to Saskatchewan, Manitoba, Nova Scotia, Prince Edward Island, New Brunswick, Newfoundland and Labrador, along with the territories, to try to work out some reasonable deal, and this we did on many occasions.

When I was chair of the Provincial-Territorial Finance ministers, we managed to get an agreement out of Ottawa that the provinces had never been able to get before. That is, we got them to agree that we could have our own income tax systems, though Ottawa would still administer the provincial systems. This agreement led to the ability of Saskatchewan and other provinces to substantially reform their income tax systems, as Alberta and Saskatchewan subsequently did. Before this change, provinces other than Quebec, which exercises its right to collect its own taxes, could only charge a percentage of federal tax. For example, our Saskatchewan income tax was, at one time, fifty percent of the federal tax. This was called the "tax-on-tax" system. After the change, we could design our own tax system — the "tax-on-income" system. This enabled us to design a system which would be tailored to meet Saskatchewan's priorities and build our economy. The tax reform that we implemented from 1999 to 2003 not only substantially reduced income taxes for Saskatchewan families, but also allowed us to offer, for example, a seniors' tax credit and the universal child tax credit. In 2007, the finance minister was able to introduce a special credit for graduates of universities or technical schools who decided to work in Saskatchewan. These measures not only benefit families here in many ways their government is sensitive to, but also help focus on measures that can encourage people to live, work and invest in Saskatchewan.

This development required a lot of discussion and negotiation with the federal government. While this agreement on income tax is a striking example of what the federal-provincial-territorial ministers' meetings could accomplish, these meetings produced many other arrangements between Ottawa and the provinces and territories as well.

In addition to setting the stage for personal income tax reform, another issue that provoked the NDP government into action and was a continuing priority during my time as Finance minister was the enhancement of Saskatchewan's credit rating.

During this time, Saskatchewan continued to receive credit rating upgrades from Canadian and international credit rating agencies. We continued to cut taxes while, at the same time, reducing our debt-to-GDP ratio. In fact, Saskatchewan has received sixteen credit rating upgrades since 1995.

Straight "A" credit ratings and an improved debt situation did not, of course, stop right-wing political editorialists at the *Saskatoon StarPhoenix* and a few other political columnists from their non-stop, often nonsensical ranting and raving about NDP fiscal policies. After a while, you realize it is largely political ranting. Sometimes, though, it is personal and mean spirited. Mostly it is seemingly irreversible and not worth paying much attention to. It's like one of the legislature's security people remarked to me about a long speech being delivered by an MLA. "It's like wiping your ass with a hoola-hoop," he told me: "There's just no end to it!"

I once heard a story about Roy Romanow walking his dog. He was throwing a stick, which the dog was fetching. He accidentally threw the stick into the South Saskatchewan River. The dog actually walked on water to retrieve the stick. The next day, the *StarPhoenix* headline read "Romanow's Dog Can't Swim".

Sometimes it did seem that no matter how successful the province was moving forward fiscally or economically, or what gains had been made under the NDP, its critics and some press pundits wore blinders and refused to recognize any progress. If things were bad, it was the NDP's fault. If things were good, they said it had nothing to do with the NDP. Nevertheless, the work must continue with or without the acknowledgements.

Toward the end of the 1990's, I realized that balancing the budget and improving the province's credit rating were largely attained. It was time for new priorities. During the first term of NDP government (1991-95), we were mainly engaged in the war on the deficit. As well, health reform was a major file.

The war on the deficit had been won, and it had been exhausting. In addition, the concentration on the deficit prevented us from working on other files. We needed new, focused goals. As well, on a personal level, I always wanted to have an agenda of things to be worked on that could make a difference in Saskatchewan people's lives. What were the most important things we should be trying to accomplish? What contribution could I make?

It is fair to say that, in fighting the fiscal deficit, other deficits arose, and were lurking. There were the needs of the municipalities, whose funding had been cut back in the first term. New schools, school repairs and new university buildings were needed. Highways were in disrepair. All of these issues, and more, needed attention, planning and action. Of course, not everything can be done at once, and deciding what should take precedence would not be easy. But I did feel, as Finance minister, my role would be to try to lead us forward in a few major policy areas. If we couldn't fix everything, we could at least begin to fix some of these urgent problems. In retrospect this decision turned out to be expensive, but also necessary.

First, I set out to convince my colleagues we needed to give the public reasons to re-elect the NDP government in 1999 and that in shaping public policy two pressing issues had to be addressed: the state of the highways, and high personal income taxes. The first of these issues was straightforward. The highways budget had been reduced to the point where the roads just weren't maintained effectively. They were time-expired and a growing mess. Questions in question period showed that the state of highways was a real public concern. The other issue of orchestrating tax cuts on personal income was not so straightforward. It would take me down a path that I would later learn was one of my most difficult and controversial.

In the fall of 1998 we had some money, and I recommended to the Treasury Board, which recommended to cabinet, that we announce a three-year plan to fix the roads. We would spend 300 million dollars per year for three years. The theme, which I suggested, was quite simple: "We're fixing the roads." It certainly was what people wanted and, after they saw work begin, the political noise and legislative questions about this issue faded away.

That initial three-year plan was ultimately replaced by a second three-year plan. The theme was amended to "We're building better roads" at some point. No doubt a very able communications consultant was engaged for the purpose.

Around the time of the "fixing the roads" plan, it struck me that anything worthwhile and significant takes a long time to accomplish. You can't fix a broken highways system overnight. You need a multi-year plan, and a long-term vision — not always guaranteed in politics.

Certainly I had seen this as a result of the "building independence" plan that was introduced as part of my first (1998-99) budget. This plan, devised by the Department of Social Services under Bob Pringle and Lorne Calvert was simple, sensible and effective, but it took a number of years for its important work to bear fruit.

The independence plan was, and remains, that working poor families with children should not have less money than people on welfare. It is not hard to see that a single mother on welfare with kids who need dental care, eyeglasses and medication cannot go to work for less money and, at the same time, lose health coverage previously provided by welfare to pay for things that her children need. The old rules prevented people from leaving social assistance and becoming independent.

The new rules allowed people to move off welfare and maintain certain benefits. It worked. Thousands of families have moved off welfare under the plan, which is what people want to do if they can. Because of such change, the number of people living on social assistance in Saskatchewan has been greatly reduced. This is due both to an improved economy and social policies that do not discourage people from going into the work force. As the "building independence" long-term plan had born results, I knew the "we're fixing the roads" plan would do the same. But what remained was the issue of high personal income tax.

By 1999, I was convinced that Saskatchewan had to have a new provincial income tax system. I had worked as chair of the Provincial-Territorial Finance ministers to have the right to implement a new system. I felt that our old provincial income tax system, with its regressive flat tax, unrealistic high-income surtax, debt reduction surtax and high rates, was not serving the people well. That is when the idea for personal income tax reform became a personal priority and gave me another mission as a politician.

From 1991 to 1995, the mission of government was "slaying the deficit monster". The government of 1995 to 1999 involved regrouping and setting new priorities. In the 1999 provincial election, I told constituents that my priority, if re-elected, would be to rewrite the income tax system, to accomplish our party's platform commitment to reduce the "average" family's income taxes by $1,000 per year. This goal, eventually, was exceeded. By the 2003 election, my new pledge would be to focus on changes that would encourage economic development and jobs, but, in 1999, my priority was personal income tax reform.

Abolishing the old income tax system and replacing it with a new provincial income tax system was a major under-taking. To this day, there are those in the NDP and the labour movement who oppose the income tax reform that was brought in between 1999 and 2003, although the number of opponents has dramatically diminished, since the vast majority of members of the public and the party support the changes that have been made. They have seen the new system work.

In the 1999-2000 Budget Speech, I announced to the legislature that a committee would be appointed which would examine Saskatchewan's personal income tax system. I said that that committee would present a report in the fall of 1999, that that report would be made public, and that the government would outline, in the 2000-2001 budget speech, a plan to bring in a new system of personal income tax for Saskatchewan. And this is what we did.

The Personal Income Tax Review Committee was composed of three accountants, namely Jack Vicq, Charlie Baldock and Shelley Brown. It came to be known as the "Vicq Committee." It recommended sweeping changes, and a new system, which would reduce income tax revenue to the provincial government by over 430 million dollars per year, offset by sales tax expansion of about 180 million dollars per year, for an approximate loss to tax revenue of around a quarter of a billion dollars each year. The "tax-on-tax" system would be replaced by a Saskatchewan-focused "tax-on-income" system.

Opponents argued that this loss to tax revenue could be used to pay for important and needed health, education and social programs. But economic revision never comes easy. With every radical change in public policy, opposition will always state the obvious and offer the public a reason to doubt any progress.

So, why did we do it? Why did a social democratic government implement the largest tax cuts in Saskatchewan's history?

I pause here to note that, between the budget promise of tax reform made in the March, 1999 budget and the budget speech that followed for 2000-2001, the 1999 election had occurred. This began with most people predicting an easy third-term majority win for Roy Romanow and the New Democrats, but this was not to be. In fact, if my colleagues and I felt a bit fatigued by deficit fighting, many NDP voters felt it too. They stayed home in droves, as the numbers showed on election night. I think voters felt that the NDP was correcting mistakes of the past, but they wanted a hopeful vision of the future. NDP voters came back, however, in 2003, when the election gave, by then NDP leader, Premier Lorne Calvert the majority denied Roy Romanow in 1999.

The 1999 near-defeat, which resulted in a minority government for the NDP, was an unpleasant surprise. The day after the election, I sat down with Premier Romanow, his assistant, the late Bill Rybotycki, and a few others including Dwain Lingenfelter to discuss strategy.

Here was an opportunity to see two political wizards at work, namely Roy and Dwain. Although the NDP was reduced to a minority, and had garnered fewer votes than the conservative Saskatchewan Party led by Elwin Hermanson, Roy Romanow and Dwain Lingenfelter were not about to turn over the keys to the Saskatchewan legislature. They immediately decided to approach the Liberals, who held the balance of power with three seats, to form a workable coalition government.

I must admit, I didn't think it would work. I didn't think the Liberals would go for it. And, I didn't know how other

New Democrats would feel about getting into bed with the Liberals. But I was wrong. With Dwain taking a lead role in discussions with Liberal leader Jim Melenchuk and Liberal MLAs Jack Hillson and Ron Osika, preliminary discussions led to meetings involving the premier. An agreement was arrived at. While some people think the Liberals were unwise to give up their balance of power by entering a coalition with the NDP, I think it is fair to say that an early election would have squeezed them out of the legislature, as ultimately happened in 2003. As well, these three particular MLAs really were more comfortable with NDP government than the right wing Saskatchewan Party, which, after all, is a "kissing cousin" of the federal Conservatives, who are the natural opponents of the federal Liberals. Thus, the NDP, as the enemy of their enemy, was really their nearest friend.

In any event, Jim Melenchuk, Ron Osika and Jack Hillson proved to be skilled ministers in the coalition government. Ron Osika also became an effective and respected Speaker of the House. In fact, speaking of Speakers, I found all of the Speakers elected by the house — the no-nonsense Herman Rolfes, the affable Glenn Hagel, Ron Osika and eventually the even-handed Myron Kowalsky — to be scrupulously fair and non-partisan in their rulings. On one occasion the Speaker asked me to withdraw remarks and apologize to the house, which I did. In answering questions from Elwin Hermanson, I had called him and his party a bunch of "phony baloney hypocrites" and they complained to the speaker about my language. I don't know if they objected to the "phony", the "baloney" or the "hypocrites" part, probably a combination of the three. On another occasion, the usually mild-mannered Melfort MLA Rod Gantefoer got kicked out for calling me a liar, one of a list of forbidden words. For his efforts he made the six o'clock TV news, which I suppose was all he really wanted.

I had got to know Liberals Ron Osika and Buckley Belanger (later elected as an NDP member) quite well while they were in opposition under Lynda Haverstock. She, of course, later became the victim of a "palace revolt" by the Liberals and resigned as Liberal leader.

Lynda Haverstock is a complex personality. Intelligent, assertive, and confident in her opinions, she is probably more suited to vice-regal authority, which is undisputed, than she was to trying to lead, in a collegial manner, the usually dysfunctional Saskatchewan Liberal party. I think Lynda Haverstock performed amazingly well as leader of the Saskatchewan Liberals. In the 1991 election, where, of course, the electorate's focus was to rid Saskatchewan of the Devine Conservatives, she managed to win the Saskatoon Greystone seat by defeating Peter Prebble, a very able and experienced NDP campaigner. Then, in the 1995 election, she led the Liberals to official opposition status, supplanting the Conservatives, who elected five members. The Liberals had eleven seats, and had obtained thirty-five per cent of the vote, up from one seat and twenty-four percent in 1991. They should have appreciated Lynda's accomplishments as leader. No other Liberal leader had obtained such results in decades. They should have planned, and worked, to replace the NDP as government. They were poised to do so.

Yet, less than two years after the 1995 election, the Saskatchewan Liberal party suddenly imploded, and Lynda left to sit as an independent. Of course, it is difficult from the outside to know everything that led to this result. Knowing some of the personalities from the inside, however, my guess is that there were too many competing large egos and forceful, if not always convincing, personalities. Lynda herself, while very able, probably did not suffer fools within the Liberal caucus very gladly, and she certainly had her share of those to deal with. One such personality was Glen McPherson who had left the NDP over health policy, and was then a Liberal MLA. Later, he would seek a Canadian Alliance federal nomination. He had demonstrated that loyalty to a leader or party was not crucial to him and, having taken him into the Liberal fold, Lynda would eventually see him undermine her, just as he had proved disloyal to Roy Romanow, his former leader.

Insider thinking was that other members of the Liberal caucus were probably more "anti-NDP" than actual Liberals. They wanted power. And, they wanted it quickly. If this could not be delivered in a hurry, they were not prepared to sit around and support their party leader or any particular set of principles. They ultimately joined with Conservative MLAs to form the Saskatchewan Party in 1997.

This development must have had Progressive Conservative leader Bill Boyd "laughing all the way to the bank". He had taken over the scandal-ridden Saskatchewan Progressive Conservatives months before the 1995 election. When I met him on the steps of the legislature a few days after he became leader, I congratulated him.

"I don't know why you're congratulating me," he said. "We'll be lucky if we win two seats." But by clever targeting to the most right-wing constituencies, in fact Bill brought them back with five seats after the 1995 election. Given the public anger at the Conservatives over the fiscal situation and the scandals emerging in their wake, this was truly remarkable.

But the icing on the cake for Bill and his colleagues was that they were able to co-opt most of the larger Liberal caucus elected in 1995 into the Saskatchewan Party which is, of course, really the Conservative Party in disguise. Or, as some would put it, it is simply in its own "witness protection program".

The Saskatchewan Liberal party has not as yet recovered from these turbulent developments. Some Liberals remained loyal to the Liberal cause after Lynda was dumped, and after most of their colleagues joined up with the Conservatives. Ron Osika and Buckley Belanger were the only two Liberal MLAs re-elected, and Liberal leader Jim Melenchuk, elected in Saskatoon Northwest in the 1999 provincial election, joined them. For many, though, it was the end of their allegiance to the Liberal Party.

As mentioned, I thought Ron and Buckley to be very companionable, and we all became good friends. In fact, we seemed to enjoy each other's company so much that we spent one entire night talking over "a few" beers in the Liberal caucus office about colleagues we all disliked, Buckley's "alleged" athletic prowess as a hockey player and the big picture of Saskatchewan politics. The next morning, around 7:00 AM, we were taken for breakfast by one of the legislature's friendly and helpful Commissionaires. He astutely observed that we were in need of some food after the night's activities. It seems fitting that, later, Buckley resigned his seat in Athabasca to run for the NDP. He was elected as a New Democrat with ninety-four percent of the vote, which must be something of a record. After serving as Speaker of the House, Ron Osika became an able cabinet minister in the NDP-Liberal coalition government of 1999-2003.

With the formation of a coalition government after the 1999 election, Ron, Buckley and I all sat on the same side of the House, but we never did get together for drinks again, which is probably just as well. Buckley, who has a good sense of humour, is quite fond of telling people about his notable achievements as a hockey player and generally trying to get a rise out of anyone he is talking to. One day I had a chance to give him some of his own when he told me that I was probably wondering why he married his charming and pretty wife Beckie. "No, Buckley," I said. "Actually, we were all wondering why Beckie would marry you." When Buckley and I were somewhere together, I used to generate interest by introducing Buckley and mentioning that he had played hockey for Boston. Once that had their attention, I would say "Well, Boston Pizza, actually." Politics can generate some atypical friendships and Buckley was one.

The Liberals who served in the NDP-Liberal coalition government of 1999-2003 welcomed personal income tax reform. Up to that time, Saskatchewan had the second highest income taxes in Canada, second only to Quebec. There was already a difference between our taxes and Alberta's, and this was one factor in Saskatchewan's out-migration. But, the difference was about to get bigger, because Alberta had just introduced its new flat tax as part of its new provincial personal income tax system. This substantially lowered its personal income taxes even more. Being one of its closest neighbours, Saskatchewan noticed.

I did not promote income tax reform and reduction as my major goal for the third term of NDP government out of any sympathy for the right wing philosophy of the Canadian Taxpayers' Federation and their supporters. I am not a tax-cutting Conservative. Nor do I believe, as they do, that "the best government is the least government". My motivation in tax reform was to achieve greater fairness and equality for Saskatchewan citizens and, at the same time, get rid of the most glaring irritants of the former Saskatchewan personal income tax system, which might cause some people to move to Alberta.

Before I entered politics, Pauline and I both had well-paying professional jobs. We each would often say to one another that we did not mind paying the income taxes we paid. Firstly, they were not outrageous. Secondly, we both appreciated the fact that the taxpayers had paid for our K-12 schooling and most of our university educations. Our families could not have afforded to pay for this. I often say to people who complain about the level of taxation in Saskatchewan and Canada that, if they moved to places like Haiti or Rwanda, they would not have to worry about income taxes. They would have no tax system in place. Places like that, however, are impoverished with no systems of education or health care for the vast majority of people. Nor do they have good economies.

Surely, that is the point. You get what you pay for, and you can't expect roads and education and medical care unless you are prepared to pay for it. As well, we need to remind ourselves that we are very privileged members of the world community. We are lucky to live in Canada. We are incredibly well off compared to just about everyone else in the world. Those who complain about taxes should really give their heads a shake.

One day I was campaigning in the Dundonald neighbourhood in Saskatoon when the man of the house greeted me at the door by proceeding to yell at me. "Do you know," he shouted "I paid $14,000 in f—g taxes last year." I listened to him vent for a while before I spoke.

"You have three children in school," I said. "If you lived in the US you would be spending at least $10,000 on healthcare premiums. It would cost you $5,000 per year to educate each of your kids. So, guess what, using their scale you owe Canada another $11,000," I informed him.

Sometimes people surprise you. This guy was not stupid, but he had never really thought about the benefits of living here. He calmly looked at me. "You're right," he actually said. He then told me that he was going to vote for me, as he had before.

I have never been afraid to defend taxation. In fact, it is, contrary to popular belief and right-wing mythology, part of the price we pay to live in a civilized society. Countries with no organized tax system are also the most backward. Paying for systems together that few or none of us can afford ourselves moves all of us forward together. We become more educated, healthier and mobile professionally and personally. We also have stronger economies because of healthier, more educated populations, and effectively develop such things as transportation and information infrastructure.

The benefits of taxation are rarely spoken of; the mindless complaints about it persist. At the doorstep, people come up with all kinds of reasons why they should not pay school taxes on their property. These include: "I have no kids, therefore I should not pay school taxes.", "My kids have finished school, therefore I should not pay school taxes.", "I am a senior, therefore I should not pay school taxes.", "I own more than one property, therefore I should not pay school taxes on each one.", "I have a low income, therefore I should not pay school taxes."

When you hear these excuses, you have to reason with people. You remind them that they, and possibly their grown children, received an education through government and school boards that they could not have received if their family had to pay for it. That is why we have public education. The cost of that education is spread throughout society and we amortize the cost of our education throughout our entire lives. We need to pay for it, and celebrate it. The education system benefits us each individually if we take advantage of it. It benefits all of us as a society to live in a well-educated environment. You have to remind people that sometimes they take too much for granted.

So, on a philosophical level, I am not anti-tax. I am very much in favour of paying a fair share of taxes to live in a fair and civilized society. Nor do I see the acquisition of wealth as my primary motivator. These are fundamental beliefs and explain why I am a social democrat. I was very pleased when Si Halyk's secretary Valerie Makela reported to me that Si had said I was one of the few people he knew who was "not motivated by money." I considered this a major compliment.

The fact is, however, that no tax system is perfect, and a balanced approach is needed. Just as it is wrong to want solely to earn the most money and pay the least amount of tax, so, too, it is wrong to ignore the reality that acquisition of wealth and income is a motivating factor for people, and incentives need to exist to drive people to work hard, build enterprises and provide employment.

This is not rocket science. One can be a social democrat believing in collective financing of various public systems, utilities, and sometimes enterprises, while recognizing the value of a market economy that allows people to pursue the profit motive. The two can certainly go together and, in fact, logically should go together.

The private economy needs public education to train its workforce and it needs the Medicare system to provide healthy people and minimize benefits costs. It is no surprise that the "big three" automakers have urged the federal government to maintain the public Medicare system. It gives them a cost advantage that they do not have with their US plants, given the backward and inequitable US health-care system. The private sector also needs public infrastructure like roads to move goods efficiently. The public sector, at the same time, needs a healthy private sector to produce the wealth and pay the taxes that will allow for the necessary public system to be paid for. This inter-dependence requires a balanced approach that recognizes the value, fairness and utility of taxes while also encouraging hard work and the entrepreneurship that is necessary for society to work well. After thinking about it for years, I've concluded that the ideal political party would seek a society which values personal freedom, promotes the market economy, and recognizes the role government can play to achieve equality of opportunity and social solidarity.

As mentioned earlier, Saskatchewan had the second highest personal income taxes in Canada prior to 2000. Being next to Alberta, which, of course, has the lowest, presents a problem. People can be motivated to move to another province for tax reasons. In fact, many high-income people do move. When people leave one province for another, it is a loss to the province and to the public treasury.

It is true that young people do not leave Saskatchewan for lower taxes. They leave for job opportunities, if they have to. This has occurred in Saskatchewan and other provinces for many decades. It is what politicians work to try to reverse. In this situation too, taxation levels will play a part in determining what the job opportunities are.

As Saskatchewan's Finance minister, I watched very closely when, in early 1999, Alberta, which already had the lowest personal income taxes in Canada, announced that it would move to a new "flat" income tax system the next year. If Saskatchewan stood still, basically Alberta's income taxes, with their new system, would be about half as much as ours. The difference would be huge. One can imagine thousands of retired people with pension income, including teachers and nurses with public sector pensions, looking over the border. They are not disloyal people, but if a simple move means taxes are cut in half, does anyone really think they won't consider it, or that many won't go?

Noteworthy as well was the certainty that Alberta's new system would be much fairer and more progressive for low-income taxpayers than Saskatchewan's former system would be. Under Alberta's new flat tax system, generous personal and family exemptions would mean families would start paying income tax at around $30,000. Not only would Alberta's new system be good for the rich, it would be much more fair for low-income people. Thanks in large part to the flat tax imposed by the Devine Conservative government in the '80s, Saskatchewan started taxing senior citizens at around $12,000 and families with kids at about $15,000. Contrary to their endless rants about fiscal responsibility, no one seemed to cause deficits and higher taxes more frequently than Saskatchewan Conservatives, and now with this alarming comparison with our provincial neighbour, the tax gap was astonishingly wide.

Given this scenario, I advised my colleagues that something had to be done in a timely way. We needed change, and we needed it fast. A combination of political will, the full support of Premier Romanow, the work of deputy Finance minister Bill Jones and an excellent team of public servants at the taxation and intergovernmental affairs division of the Department of Finance — Kirk McGregor, Eric Johnson,

Arun Srinivas and Nathan Dvernichuk — and the good advice of the Vicq Committee all contributed to this major change.

In the budget speech of spring 1999, I announced that the Personal Income Tax Review Committee would be named, that it would fully examine Saskatchewan's system of personal taxation, that it would report to government that year, that the report would be made public and that the government would introduce a new personal taxation system the following year.

There is no doubt that the 2000 budget had to prescribe a new system. That is what we promised, and that is what we had to deliver. The vision for tax reform had commitment, it had a committee, but like all successful long term plans, it had obstacles to overcome and a way to go to become reality.

First Nations People and Taxes

QUITE UNDERSTANDABLY, PEOPLE FEEL THAT everyone benefits from public programs, and, therefore, everyone should pay taxes to support them. However, there is a great deal of frustration among non-First Nations people who hold the perception that "Indians don't pay taxes". In fact, this is largely untrue. In order to understand why it is untrue, some knowledge of both federal and provincial tax law needs to be clarified. Under *The Indian Act*, a law of the federal government, First Nations people cannot be taxed on reserve. Therefore, if they purchase items on reserve, or work on reserve for a First Nations organization, they are not subject to federal or provincial taxation. This law exists because the reserves are their land, left to them after they ceded most of the rest of Canada to the Europeans represented by the Crown. Not a bad bargain. If they live or work off reserve, they pay taxes like everyone else. If they own or rent a home off reserve, they pay property taxes directly or indirectly. If they work off reserve, they pay income taxes like everyone else. If they buy gas off reserve, they pay gas taxes.

Prior to the 2000 budget, which I delivered, First Nations people did not pay provincial sales tax (PST) on off-reserve purchases. If they presented their treaty card number making the purchase, the tax was removed. This was a major irritant to the majority of the population, sometimes lined up at the tills, while the tax was deducted. It created animosity, and contributed to the false notion that, generally, "Indians don't pay taxes".

Further to this, the historical tax trade-off between the province and band councils was being legally questioned and so one of the issues dealt with alongside personal income tax reform was First Nations and payment of PST off reserve. While the province cannot legally impose taxes on First Nations people on reserve, as mentioned, we did impose all other taxes off reserve, except the PST. The trade-off, historically, had been that we collected tobacco tax and gas tax for on-reserve purchases by First Nations people. First Nations people were in the courts through their band councils, however, now challenging this arrangement. There were eight or nine lawsuits against the government for collecting gas and tobacco taxes from First Nations people on reserve, and the advice I received from government lawyers was that we would lose these lawsuits. Manitoba had already lost a lawsuit over the same issue, and was paying millions of dollars in compensation. The legal consensus was that the provincial government was already liable to pay over $20 million dollars back to the First Nations, and, if we didn't stop collecting gas and tobacco tax on reserve, the liability would become larger. More and more businesses were being established on reserve and, therefore, First Nations people were being charged more and more gas and tobacco taxes, illegally, on purchases.

Since the historic trade-off of not charging PST off reserve but taxing certain items on reserve was no longer left unchallenged, it was time for change. We made the decision to respect the letter of the tax law on reserve, rebating all tax paid by First Nations people back to First Nations, but established the imposed collection of PST from First Nations people off reserve, which we had the legal right to do. First Nations leaders, led by FSIN Chief Perry Bellegarde, expressed their opposition to the change, since new tax is never popular with anyone and certainly wasn't with First Nations people. They said it contravened treaty rights, and commenced legal action, which has never been actively pursued since being initiated in 2000. Whether this legal action will proceed at some future date seems less and less likely, as the new law did strike a note of fairness.

In addition to being in compliance with federal law, imposition of PST off reserve had the advantage that it encouraged economic development on reserve. Since the province cannot impose PST on reserve, First Nations people move their business to First Nations land to take advantage of their legal entitlement. As well, there are an increasing number of First Nations entrepreneurs, which is a healthy development. Business has developed on reserve as a result. For many years, there were communities on reserve of hundreds of people, and no business activity. All the shopping went to the nearby town. Now reserves began to provide more services and the money generated stayed on the reserve. We would not think it was a satisfactory state of affairs to see a town of several hundred people with no businesses locally owned and there to serve the local people. Why was it ever satisfactory for that state of affairs to exist on reserve? So, economic change began to happen and continues to do so.

Of course, not everyone saw this coming. Before the tax changes, I went to a meeting in a small Saskatchewan town to meet the local Chamber of Commerce. One of their big complaints was that "Indians don't pay sales tax". When was I going to make everyone "equal"? "Be careful what you wish for," I said. "Because one of these days, we will impose PST on everyone, but, by law, we can't do so on reserve." I explained further that more and more business will move to the reserve, and the patronage they previously enjoyed would be diminished. That trend has now begun, and while some towns did lose this customer base, I believe the overall fabric of Saskatchewan was strengthened as more First Nations businesses started and succeeded. While fairness and parity have always been the buzz words associated with First Nations people and tax law changes, as we have more economic development by First Nations people, we will, in fact, have more equality in our society.

Organizations like the Saskatchewan Indian Gaming Authority (SIGA) have greatly enhanced the economic well-being of Saskatchewan First Nations people, and, therefore, the province as a whole, by providing employment to hundreds of Aboriginal people and demonstrating economic leadership. First Nations like the Whitecap Dakota and Lac La Ronge Indian Bands have greatly contributed to improvement of economic status by starting First Nations enterprises, whether they are golf courses, trucking enterprises or otherwise. SIGA itself has become a multi-million dollar organization through its casinos. Ultimately, such economic activity spread fairly and effectively throughout the province will result in more social equality and tax fairness for all Saskatchewan people.

Personal Life Reminders

THE ELECTED REPRESENTATIVE'S LIFE DEMANDS endless hours of work, and that increases in the role of a minister. While I never lost sight of how important my private life was, and how much my family meant to me, there are always reminders along the way that drive that message home.

I was busily preparing to deliver the 2000 budget, always a hectic time but especially so when a big change is planned. Five days before budget day, my stepfather Al Vance died in his sleep. This event pulled me back into my personal life even though I had pressing work to do. The demands of the job sometimes make politicians put their lives on hold, but we may be grounded by personal realities when we least expect it.

My father died in 1976 when I was a third-year university student. My mother remarried seven years later, in 1983, but she died suddenly of a heart attack in 1986. My stepfather Al had been left alone. He had been widowed once before, and had no children, although he was close to two nephews, his sister and nieces. Al was a colourful character who had worked as a farmer, trapper and carpenter. After my mom's death, we remained close, and he was a regular visitor to our home. Pauline, who had lost both of her parents by the age of twelve, enjoyed Al's company as well. Throughout the years, Al was a regular visitor and our relationship with him was close.

In the mid-1990s, as Health minister, I had often listened to the concerns of adult children with elderly parents. Problems with legal affairs, getting home care, hospitalization, nursing home care and access to personal care homes were all issues. As Al got older, I became familiar with all these issues on a personal basis. He grew progressively more unable to take care of his medication, meals and personal affairs. It was with some trepidation that I approached him one day around 1997 and said I thought he needed to sign a Power of Attorney so I, or some other relative, could take care of the rent, bills, and generally be there as an advisor. Because Al had always been a proud and independent person, I dreaded this conversation. So I was quite surprised when his reaction was, "Good! You take over!" He was pleased and obviously relieved. I guess he was having some difficulties, but wasn't about to ask for help.

Thereafter, I took care of Al's affairs. Although I was busy between Regina and Saskatoon, Pauline bought Al's groceries and visited his apartment regularly to make sure he was taken care of and taking his pills. I really appreciated the care and concern extended to Al by people in his later years, as well as the excellent service provided by the home care system of the Saskatoon Health District. It was rewarding as Health minister to see that our system really worked.

As Al progressed from his own apartment to seniors' public housing, in and out of hospital and into a personal care home, I developed strong empathy for all caregivers. I also came to appreciate home care services, public housing and the Saskatoon Housing Authority immensely. Like my dad, Al was a decorated veteran of World War II, and I was very happy with the assistance extended by the Department of Veterans' Affairs as well. It was fitting that, for those who gave to their country, in the end their country could give something back.

When Al died shortly before budget day in 2000, I was the executor of his estate, so it was my responsibility to make the funeral arrangements. At the same time, it was my responsibility to make many final arrangements for budget day. Budget week is the busiest time of the year for the Finance minister. As well, the coalition government had only a few more seats than the opposition, and MLAs couldn't be away from the legislature when it was in session.

I arranged for the funeral to take place in Saskatoon the morning before the budget speech, and went back and forth between Saskatoon and Regina, attending to funeral arrangements and visiting family and friends in Saskatoon, while leading my colleagues through the budget package in Regina.

It was a very difficult week for me but, as many experience when you simply have to do things, you do them. Afterwards, you often collapse with illness like the flu as soon as the events are over and adrenalin stops running, which is exactly what I did after burying my stepfather and the next day delivering the budget speech in that awful week in March 2000.

Political Vision To Political Reality:
Tax Reform

THE VICQ COMMITTEE HAD PROVIDED AN EXCELLENT report upon which to base the new system of personal income taxation that was announced in the 2000-2001 budget speech. It was not "pie in the sky." It was doable from a practical point of view, and it was politically saleable.

Of course, critics on both the right and the left lined up to take pot shots at the report, which is their right, and contributes to public debate. On the right, critics said the Committee was wrong to recommend that sales taxes be expanded to raise revenue to pay for massive cuts to personal income taxes. They wanted much lower income taxes, but all of the tax cut was to be paid for by cuts to government spending. When I asked them to identify where spending should be cut, however, they would never specify. Was it in health care? Was it in education? Health and education consume sixty percent of provincial government spending. Was it in highways? Or, was it in agriculture? Of course, they had no answer and since no suggestions were forthcoming, the right wing criticism of the report was hard to take seriously.

On the left, led by the Saskatchewan Federation of Labour (SFL), the criticism was that lowering income taxes would mainly benefit "the rich" or, at the very least, would benefit the well-to-do more than the middle and lower income people. Their position was that tax cuts for well-off people were wrong, as they could "afford to pay".

I went to countless meetings where I met this criticism, but I never wavered in my commitment to personal income tax reform. The fact is that Saskatchewan has few "rich" people. Middle-income people pay the brunt of personal income taxes, and they demanded and deserved reform. I tried to explain to the leaders of the SFL that I had been on more doorsteps of union members than they had, and that, whether they believed it or not, the average steelworker working in the mines was demanding lower income taxes. That is what rank and file union members wanted.

In fact, at a meeting of the Saskatoon Labour Council in January 2000, I was asked to speak and to answer questions. One by one the union leaders came to the microphones and explained that my views were misguided. The general theme, they insisted, should be to "make the rich pay." They did not want to hear about how this income tax reform could be beneficial to all the people of Saskatchewan.

I pointed out to the meeting that there were members or the United Steelworkers of America working in northern Saskatchewan uranium mines, flying out to Saskatoon and then driving to their homes in Lloydminster, Alberta, so that they could have lower income taxes and keep more of their hard-earned money. I was not aware at the time, but found out later, that several of these steelworkers were present at the meeting, en route from the north to Lloydminster to which they would escape after the meeting. They apparently made it known to some of their brothers and sisters that what I was saying was, in fact, true. The discrepancy between Saskatchewan and Alberta personal income taxes was too large to ignore.

Finally, one lone ranger union representative approached the microphone to come to my defence. Greg Eyre, then a staff representative of the United Food and Commercial Workers in Saskatoon, made it known that the views of the union leadership did not reflect all the views of the rank and file, in his opinion. He said that his members wanted public services, but also wanted lower income taxes. I admired his candour and his courage.

Another interesting aside to the debate was that the Vicq Committee recommended that we apply the sales tax to certain forms of contract income. It turned out that one or two of the labour leaders who worked for unions were on contract rather than salary. Previously this had reduced their income taxes, since they worked as "consultants". On the one hand, they complained publicly that income taxes should not be lowered, while, privately, a few of them arranged their own affairs to minimize the income tax they paid. They were concerned that an expansion of the sales tax might apply to their earnings. What people say and do are often two very different realities, and every time I feel I have heard it all, something else comes along. I hasten to add, however, that while I disagreed with the majority of labour leaders who opposed income tax reform, their motivation in opposing it was a sincerely held view that it could jeopardize programs for ordinary people.

In the budget of 2000, a plan to implement the largest tax reduction and tax reform in Saskatchewan's history was set out. Like any worthwhile and significant effort, it would take time. The plan would begin in 2000, with expansion of the sales tax as of budget day. A series of personal income tax cuts would start on July 1, 2000, and continue until 2004.

In the main, we implemented the Vicq Report, but made some changes. We would reduce income taxes by more than a third between 2000 and 2004, but we would not reduce the provincial sales tax from six percent to five percent as the committee recommended. The reason for this was that, in order for the PST to go to five percent, the committee recommended that the sales tax be applied to several things that I, and the government, felt it should not be applied to. People, generally, felt that the major impasse was the committee's recommendation that the PST be applied to restaurant meals, but this wasn't the major problem. The main problem we had was with the breadth of the proposed PST expansion. For example, the committee had recommended that the PST be applied to home electricity and heating charges and also the use of natural gas by business. I spoke to Jack Vicq and explained our view that to tax home heating and electricity was really a tax on shelter, or a "necessity", which the PST in Saskatchewan had not been applied to traditionally. Further to this, the problem with taxing businesses on the use of natural gas was that many Saskatchewan industries are heavily reliant on natural gas. To tax them on that cost could hurt business, and, I felt, would lead to some business closures and job losses.

Subsequent experience with high natural gas prices demonstrated that to apply a tax as a percentage to these high costs would, indeed, be very harmful. Some businesses, including a sodium sulphate producer and alfalfa pellet plants, have closed due to high natural gas costs. To apply a further five percent cost could be devastating to some.

Jack Vicq certainly understood the problems that we had with taxing home electricity and heating costs and the use of natural gas by business. After we spoke about the matter, he felt that the decision whether to apply the PST in these instances was a judgment call. He understood the government's concern. He was pleased, however, that, in almost every other respect, government implemented the recommendations of the Vicq Committee. It only made sense that five years later, after the 2005 budget, Finance Minister Harry Van Mulligan appointed Jack Vicq, Charlie Baldock and Cheryl Shepherd to look into the business tax system. Once again a committee led by Jack Vicq would introduce ideas that would lead to sweeping business tax changes in the 2006 budget.

Sometimes, politicians are accused of never being able to look at the long term, and only making decisions that would be popular in the short term. There are examples, however, where politicians are thinking about the long term, and personal income tax reform was one of them. I knew that the budget of 2000 would not be popular, because it would involve an immediate tax increase through expansion of the provincial sales tax, while it would take three or four years for the income tax reductions to be fully implemented. But I had faith, despite the knowledge that the voters rarely look at a government's long term planning.

Public reaction to the 2000 budget was not good. From a public relations point of view, it was a disaster. To immediately increase sales taxes based on a promise to reduce personal income tax over the next four years was met with scepticism, at best. Would we keep our word? When would tax relief arrive?

I had warned my colleagues that this would be the public's reaction. But, I maintained it was the correct public policy. They listened and they supported the budget. I also told them that, as tax reform unfolded, people would see tax relief. They would compare the income tax they paid each year, over the previous year, and they would see benefits. I argued that they would come to support tax reform. But, I also cautioned, it would take time, just as it took time for a sceptical public to see that Roy Romanow's promise to eliminate the huge deficit and balance the budget came to fruition. Anything worthwhile takes time. In politics, it also takes strong political will to present a long-term plan which is unpopular in the short term, but which ultimately will work.

In fact, the opposition to the plan in 2000 faded away as tax cuts rolled in year after year. There isn't anyone in Saskatchewan politics today, on either side of the house, advocating a reversal, or major change, to personal income tax reform. Tax reform removed 55,000 taxpayers from the income tax rolls altogether, introduced the only universal child tax credit in Canada, brought in the seniors' tax credit, repealed the regressive flat tax, high income and debt reduction surtaxes. It also ended "bracket creep" — the effect inflation has on tax credits and brackets. If you do not adjust the size of these to account for inflation, you effectively raise taxes each year by the rate of inflation, but without the transparency and accountability that comes from legislative debate of tax increases.

Tax reform decreased Saskatchewan's personal income taxes from the second highest in Canada to the third or fourth lowest. And, it reduced capital gains taxes to the lowest in Canada, equivalent to that of Alberta, on the sale of farms and small businesses. This removed the necessity for people to actually move to Alberta before the disposition of these assets. Alberta was the most popular destination because, before the change, it had the lowest tax. By 2006, the right-wing Fraser Institute was able to report that Saskatchewan people paid the second lowest overall personal taxes in Canada. As well, for the first time, our average personal incomes were above the national average. We were also one of three "have" provinces in Canada, something Saskatchewan people had dreamed about and aspired to for decades. We had come a long way from the bleak days of the early nineties. And, the most important development since the 1991 election was that the general despair people felt in the early nineties had been replaced by a general sense of hope, and widespread optimism about the province's future.

In fact, on October 29, 2007, nine days before the defeat of the NDP government, CIBC World Markets, in its job quality index, reported that Saskatchewan had the highest average job quality, taking wages and taxes into account, in Canada. We had made the most progress of any province for the preceding five years and had surpassed Alberta in terms of people's ability to obtain quality work. We had come a long way.

In addition to the 2000 budget's personal income tax reform, several other business tax changes were made. A new oil and gas royalty regime was brought in late in 2002, along with a new package of incentives for mining development. Professionals were allowed to incorporate. Significantly, my five and one-half years as Finance minister also allowed me to work with my colleagues to implement welfare reform, increase municipal revenue sharing, work on the highways plan, expand "community net", a high speed internet, to communities throughout Saskatchewan, and increase education funding.

One specific highlight of these other involvements was that, after the reductions and freezes to education funding the government had been required to implement in order to balance the budget, under my tenure in Finance, we were able to provide 24% more funding to K-12 education, 23% more to the universities and 28% more to the Saskatchewan Institute of Applied Science and Technology and the regional colleges. There is no area that is more important to the province's future than training young people for professional and technical jobs. In addition to increased operating funding, there was also a crying need for more money to repair and build schools and to build more university buildings. A much more ambitious program of capital funding was under-taken in the late 1990s which allowed the education sector to proceed with school repairs, school construction and construction of buildings like the Kinesiology Building at the University of Saskatchewan, the Physical Activity Centre at the University of Regina, the replacement of science labs at the University of Saskatchewan and many more. We were able, for example, to set aside seven million dollars towards the reconstruction of the historic College Building at the University of Saskatchewan. When this officially opened in 2005, the province's centennial year, I was extremely gratified to see the results of an improved economic and fiscal situation and to view the restored splendour of one of Saskatchewan's finest heritage buildings.

With a realistic vision of what can be, and the political will to bring about change, peoples' lives can be improved. What began with the Vicq Commission culminated in benefits for the private individual, Saskatchewan business, and the social infrastructure.

On Being Human

POLITICS OCCURS IN A PRESSURE-COOKER ENVIRONMENT. Schedules and commitments are very difficult to keep. People can be mean and nasty. Tempers can flare. At the same time, opportunities arise where people give us glimpses of themselves, which affect us for life in ways they don't even realize. In the words of a Bruce Cockburn song, people sometimes "manage to shine."

Anyone who knows Roy Romanow well and has travelled with him knows that Roy has an endearing, though slightly annoying, habit of asking fellow travellers questions, then refusing to accept their answers until they accord with his wishes.

"Where do you want to go for supper?" Roy will ask, for example. "Chinese food," you may answer.

"No, you don't," Roy may reply. "You want Italian, don't you?"

Knowing Roy wants Italian, you think — fine. "Let's have Italian," you say.

"Where would you like to go?"

You answer the question. "No, you don't want to go there! What about Mama Teresa's?"

"Okay. Mama Teresa's is fine."

It is not that Roy is selfish or unpleasant in asserting his wishes. He actually believes, in the end, that it is you who has suggested the place, and he has simply gone along with your wish, while you know that Roy has managed to get exactly what he wants because he always remains in control of the situation. Of course, that is what gave him the edge in politics.

One incident of such control occurred soon after Roy became premier and I was a newly elected MLA.

By coincidence, we were both catching an Air Canada flight to Regina early one Monday morning. Roy had not yet established an apartment in Regina, and had only one set of clothes with him, namely the ones he was wearing. We sat beside one another on the plane.

After sitting down, the dance I knew already had begun.

"Would you like some coffee?" Roy asked.

"No," I said.

"Of course you would like a cup of coffee," Roy said. "Why don't you ask the flight attendant for some coffee, and, while you are at it, I will have some, too."

So, I got the flight attendant to bring us two cups of coffee.

I placed my cup of coffee on the small tray that flips down from the seat in front of me and, for reasons I can't explain, something happened which caused my knee to jerk up under the tray, causing the coffee cup to go flying into the air.

I watched as one does in these situations, in slow motion. The cup went up and turned completely upside down. The coffee came out of the cup and spilled all over Roy, who was sitting to my right. Not a single drop landed on me.

This display had to be disconcerting and embarrassing for the new premier, especially with fellow passengers watching. But watching Roy demonstrate his composure and control of the situation made me aware of just why he had been so successful as a politician.

Roy simply took the available napkins and calmly and quietly began to clean himself up. I was very embarrassed and apologized. Roy simply said it was not a big problem, and he was okay. His poise and cool-headed control would stand him in good stead in the political ring where opposition and media would continually try to panic or upset him. He rarely wavered from his self-composure.

Although the coffee incident is amusing in one sense, it taught me a lot about how to maintain a sense of calm and decorum in troublesome situations. I wish I could say that I have always displayed the same level of decorum, but being human doesn't always allow that to happen. One does not set out to embarrass oneself in politics, but occasionally we let our feelings get the best of us and behave inappropriately toward others. I know as a cabinet minister, I tried to avoid embarrassing gaffes, and, for the most part, was successful. But no one is perfect, and after one of my budgets I "lost it" at the expense of the director of the Saskatchewan Regional Parks Association.

For some time the director and his executive had been lobbying the government to increase their funding. We were paying them $75,000 per year as a grant, and this was continued in one of my budgets. The director, however, was upset since he believed and made it known that we had not listened to their pleas for more funding.

In fact, I had worked hard to find a way to make $500,000 per year available to the regional parks for capital projects. I had set up a capital fund that would provide them with two million dollars over four years. There was two million dollars new money for regional parks in the budget, and I was obviously bewildered by his charges.

Somehow the director had missed this infusion of new money, though one wonders how, and he was publicly criticizing me. This made me angry, since I had done my best to help the Regional Parks Association and it was obvious that he hadn't done his homework.

Anger often arises from hurt feelings and, in this case, I felt hurt that the director and the Association had not acknowledged that I had listened to them and, in fact, responded to their concerns. Their public criticism was uninformed, inaccurate and, in the circumstances, unfair.

Instead of doing what I normally did when feeling angry, which was to turn to my able and unflappable chief of staff, Duane Haave, to blow off steam for a while, until he figured out the best way to deal with the situation, I did what you should never do as a politician. I phoned the director and gave him a dressing down. I told him he was wrong, didn't know what he was talking about and should "get his act together."

The director took careful notes of my tirade and, the next day, my friend, the late Carl Kwiatkowski, opposition MLA for Carrot River, raised the matter in question period as an example of how ministers should not treat the public. I should have known that this was coming. Although I explained to the legislature how and why my outburst to the director of the SRPA had arisen, the damage was done. The media, afterwards, asked me if the director's transcript of what I said to him on the phone was accurate, and I admitted it was. I knew the media would make news out of the incident, but I had brought it on myself.

Although this was not any major scandal, I was extremely embarrassed by the way I had spoken to this individual. I felt awful about it. The *StarPhoenix* rightly criticized me in an editorial and, for once, I had to agree with them. I was wrong, and I was ashamed of myself. While I often apologize if I have been wrong, I did not apologize to the SRPA director, since I thought he was both uninformed and politically motivated in his actions.

A few days later, Roy Romanow phoned me at home to discuss another matter. I hadn't had the opportunity to speak with him since the incident, and he didn't raise it. After we were finished talking about the subject Roy had called about, I told him I was very sorry that I had embarrassed the government in this way. I would have accepted a dressing down from Roy, who, as I demonstrated, rarely lost his cool in public, but in a private call might have reacted quite differently, since I had brought some negative press to the party through my actions.

"Okay, don't do it again," was all he said. I wish I could say I have always been as patient and understanding with people who have worked for me.

As with all people who share similar work, there were times when all members of the legislature set aside their differences and came together like a family. Three such occasions were the sad deaths of opposition MLAs Rudi Peters, Carl Kwiatkowski and Ben Heppner. The public does not often realize that, regardless of our political battles, members of the legislature develop friendly relationships with members of other political parties. We are all elected by the public, and we have a job to do, but can be considerate and supportive of each other's commitments. In my role as a cabinet minister, I always tried to be helpful to opposition members coming to me with constituent problems. Their constituents are taxpayers, and entitled to the same respect as anyone and, therefore, those who represent them must have access to government. It is in these exchanges that opposition members can sometimes become close associates or friends. People would be surprised, for example, to know that I consider Lyle Stewart, my former opposition energy critic, to be a friend. We have shared many laughs, and more than a few beers.

I learned how to recognize that when opposition MLAs approach privately with a problem, they are not playing politics. The politics comes when they ambush the minister in question period with a problem they haven't bothered to bring to the minister's attention for a possible solution. There will always be times when opposition members do play politics. Of course, there will also be times when those in power do as well.

But the deaths of Rudi, Carl and Ben did not leave room for politics. All were well-liked individuals who served their constituents and carried their political causes with integrity. I liked them a lot, and would regularly chat with them. Rudi Peters fought courageously against cancer, and everyone was sad when he lost his battle. He had a record of service in municipal politics, was a family man, and well regarded by MLAs on both sides of the House. Ben Heppner was a committed conservative, well grounded in his deep faith, and a fearless advocate in the legislature. I visited him in the hospital shortly before he died. He spoke of going to a better place. He was at peace.

Carl Kwiatkowski's untimely passing at a young age was the greatest shock to everyone. When I heard the news of his suicide, I really didn't believe it. Here was a young, dedicated, well-liked MLA who had already made a good contribution to the physically and mentally challenged with whom he worked in and around his hometown of Porcupine Plain. It was hard to understand why this man, with much to offer and the prospect of a cabinet post in a possible new government, would end his own life. We were all touched and disturbed by Carl's passing. Were there signs we should have picked up on? Could any of us have intervened in some way? We were all reminded of the vulnerabilities and closeness of our political community. This tragic event demonstrated as much as anything that politicians are just human beings, with the same frailties, doubts and fears others may have. The public needs to remember that, and so do the politicians.

So there were at least some occasions when we put aside our differences and came together as members of the same human family. As death could unite us, people came together too, when illness struck. Whether it was Ned Shillington's long hospitalization and subsequent use of a wheelchair, or Clay Serby's cancer, the legislature showed itself to be capable of being a concerned community. Politicians who work throughout the years come to know each other well. Therefore, any member's critical illness reminds all of us that we are vulnerable. And, of course, death, whether sudden and unexpected like that of Carl Kwiatkowski, or gentler but still surprising, as in the passing in 2006 of Deputy Minister of Industry and Resources, Larry Spannier, from cancer, affirms our mortality.

Some members were, of course, closer to these individuals than others, but all in the political community gave them the respect they deserved. I don't think Ned Shillington, who served almost twenty-five years in the legislature, had a mean bone in his body. His kindness was well known, but so was his reputation for being absent-minded. This latter quality led to a bit of consternation on occasion; nevertheless, Ned was a true gentleman and much-loved constituency man, badly missed by colleagues and many constituents when he retired in 1999.

Of course, there was one scandal that plagued Ned through his active political years. This was "perogy-gate." As the story goes, Ned's wife Sonia and fellow women from Ned's constituency association raised money each year by making and selling perogies. Apparently, someone put out a circular saying you could order these perogies by calling certain telephone numbers, one of which was Ned's office, which is, of course, funded by the taxpayers and therefore off limits to fund raising campaigns. The opposition couldn't let this go by, and raised the matter in the house. Ned was amused by this, and explained that a mistake had been made, but it was the kind of fairly innocent mistake that could be made, and after all it was just perogies.

While at the YMCA in Regina a few days later, Ned mentioned that the publicity had meant that Sonia and company were unable to keep up with the orders coming in for perogies. When the whole locker room burst into laughter, I knew that Ned's reputation for honesty had survived this "scandal". The opposition would have to find something else to pin on Ned.

Had they known more intimately Ned's reputation for absent-mindedness, they may have had some real "goods" to pin on him. For example, on one occasion, he left secret cabinet documents on the roof of his car and drove away leaving the documents on the road. Fortunately, a member of the public who was also an NDP supporter had witnessed the incident and the documents were simply returned. Even politicians, especially kind ones, have guardian angels.

Ned was not the only one to misplace documents or have the protection of a guardian angel. There was the incident where Premier Lorne Calvert left his briefcase on 33rd Street in Saskatoon while talking to the media and some kids carted it off. When they realized what they had, they quickly threw it away. It was later found and returned by a young boy from Caswell School. I am sure the premier knew that fortune was smiling on him that day.

In my own experience, I think I may have one of the best stories of misplaced documents. One Friday evening in June 1997, I was leaving my constituency office in Saskatoon. I opened the trunk of my car to put something in and noticed a very large black binder. It was the same kind of book that holds cabinet documents. I couldn't remember putting it there so at first I thought I must have left a cabinet book in the trunk of my car. This surprised me, since I would not normally do that, but what else could it be?

I picked up the binder, and much to my surprise, it was the briefing book of the Honourable Allan Rock, then federal minister of Health. It had a tab for every province and territory and contained the federal government's strategy for dealing with the provinces and territories over health matters. It also contained the federal government's views on how to deal with each provincial minister of Health, including me.

But what was it doing in the trunk of my car?

I was puzzled for a few seconds. Then I realized that, earlier that day, I had met Allan Rock in downtown Saskatoon where we had discussed health care concerns. After our meeting, I drove him and his assistant to the airport. Obviously, they had placed their belongings in the trunk, but had forgotten to remove the binder. As I thought about this, a small dilemma leapt to mind: What should I do with this? I didn't want them to think that I had taken the book. I also didn't want them to think I had read, or worse yet, copied the contents. Clearly, it would be unethical to take advantage of the situation and, for the most part, I didn't. But my overwhelming curiosity about one thing got the better of me. I could not resist reading the page that described the Saskatchewan minister of Health and what to expect from him. So, I read the federal government's view on me. While it did not provide any great revelations, it was positive. It said something to the effect that I was intelligent and well informed. For a change, I actually agreed with what the feds had to say. The report had also outlined the issues they expected me to raise. They had scouted me well.

That curiosity satisfied, I returned to the question. What to do with this thing? So, I did what any minister should do in this situation. I phoned the deputy minister of Health, recently appointed Con Hnatiuk, and asked him.

Without hesitation, Con told me simply to wrap the book in paper, seal it with packing tape, sign it, put the date and time on it, and write an explanation as to how it came into my possession. He then arranged for Health Canada officials to retrieve the book from me. They were happy to do so since, apparently, frantic and harried federal health officials had been searching the Saskatoon and Toronto airports, some airplanes and other locales for several hours trying to find the book. They would have had to search all weekend if not for the fact that I happened to have to put something into my trunk. I wondered if, once they had the book back in their possession, they thought about changing their strategy with the Saskatchewan minister of Health.

But the prize-winning story of a politician's forgetfulness still belongs to Ned Shillington. One summer Monday morning in 1993, Ned came to the legislature and told some of us about his weekend. Apparently, he had been camping with his family when he decided to take the family van for a drive.

As Ned drove along, he noticed the other campers waving their hands at him. At first, he thought they were simply well-wishers who recognized him and that he was obviously a popular public figure. But then he noticed that, actually, these people were running after his van, frantically waving their arms and yelling. It was at this point that Ned remembered that he had tied the family dog to the back of the van.

One of the people running after the van was Del Robertson, president of the Saskatchewan Chamber of Commerce. Ned, as minister of Labour, was at that time embroiled in a public dispute with Del over proposed labour legislation. Now here was Ned Shillington embarrassing himself in front of Del. Ned reported to us, that, at that moment, bringing the van to a halt, he said a silent prayer. "Please, God, let me die of a heart attack, now." Of course he didn't, because tomorrow was, after all, another day to be the minister of Labour. Whatever Del Robertson may have thought of Ned at that moment was never revealed.

The next day, Ned decided to go for a ride in his boat, with the dog who, thankfully, was not hurt by the incident with the van. Ned had just put the dog in the boat when Del

Robertson came by again, and stopped to talk to Ned on the dock.

As Ned engaged in conversation with Del, he suddenly remembered that he had untied the boat, with the dog in it. He turned around to see the dog, in the boat, floating away toward the middle of the lake. Fortunately, Del, despite his opposition to Ned's labour legislation, took Ned into his boat and the two of them managed to rescue Ned's dog and boat, which just demonstrates that even Ned's toughest political opponents just had to give in to his likeable nature.

You had to love Ned. Even though the most daunting story of Ned, who was also a pilot, almost running out of gas while flying one of our colleagues in an airplane was a bit disconcerting, in the end it is Ned's kindness and commitment we all missed after his retirement.

One of the most moving stories in the political community began to unfold in early 2004 when illness came to Clay Serby in the form of cancer. Clay and his partner Trish were friends of both Pauline and I. We had visited and stayed at their Yorkton area home on several occasions. Clay and I were also veterans of the large class of MLAs elected in 1991. We had been backbenchers together and were appointed to cabinet on the same day in November 1995.

News of Clay's illness hit all of us like a ton of bricks. Our first concern was personal, for him and his family. We knew they needed privacy, he needed treatment, and he needed time to heal. I wrote to him and told him that the affairs of the province would have to be handled by the rest of us — his priority had to be his health.

With the support of his partner, his family, friends and colleagues on both sides of the house, Clay faced his first cancer challenge and came back to the legislature, a welcomed survivor who had been badly missed. During his time away, it was fortunate that Mark Wartman could step up to the plate and assume Clay's responsibilities as minister of Agriculture and Food. Mark performed his responsibilities very well, considering, as the opposition liked to point out, he is not a farmer. Maynard Sonntag also helped by assuming Mark's Highways responsibilities until Eldon Lautermilch assumed them. Clay's courage to fight cancer and make his return to politics was an inspiration to us all, a battle he had to resume in early 2007.

In the political community we witnessed other difficult events that would bring us closer together and make us realize our vulnerabilities. Ned Shillington faced his confinement to a wheelchair with the determination and dignity one would expect from him. He continued to do his work, including door-to-door canvassing, and before his retirement was regarded by other legislators as a model MLA. Ultimately, we saw similar courage displayed by Ben Heppner, MLA for Martensville, in his battle with cancer, when again, partisan rivalries give way to basic human concern for others.

Through the years, I saw courage displayed in other ways as well. When Joanne Crofford's daughter, Sunny, a young wife and mother, became terminally ill, was hospitalized and died, I was touched by her grief, having myself lost a brother to leukemia. I knew that no parent could ever be prepared to see his or her child die. It is not how the world is supposed to work. How difficult it must have been for Joanne to carry on as a cabinet minister and as a regular caregiver to her grand-daughter Serena. At the time I knew that certain members of the public were giving Joanne a rough time over a policy issue. I could only suspect that they didn't know what she was going through.

I had come to respect Joanne as an intelligent and hardworking MLA and cabinet minister with deep connections to her community in Regina. I also regarded her as a good friend and confidante. I watched her carry on under tough circumstances, and saw how strong she really could be. A few days after Sunny's packed funeral service, Joanne rose at our NDP caucus meeting to thank her colleagues for their expressions of support and sympathy. She spoke briefly, which is understandable, and ended simply by saying we should tell those close to us that we loved them. There was something heroic about her appearance that day.

Serving the needs of your party and answering to your own personal needs is always difficult to balance. Another striking example of that balance was shown by Larry Ward, who served as MLA for Estevan for one term, 1995 to 1999. During this term, the International Brotherhood of Electrical Workers was locked out of work at SaskPower and the government decided it had no option, since it was winter, but to legislate them back to work.

Whether you agree or disagree with such a government approach is not my point. Larry was a union man from Estevan and a former employee of SaskTel. These locked out IBEW workers, largely residents of Estevan, were his union brothers and, for the most part, his supporters. They also came that day to pack the galleries and observe us debate the bill that would legislate them back to work.

I'm sure that the predicament of supporting his colleagues and the government was one of the most difficult things Larry had to do in his career. He stood up, and spoke calmly and clearly as his brothers stared down at him. He didn't duck the issue, keep quiet or abstain from voting. He did what he had to do as an elected member of a political party, and I was very impressed with the courageous and honorable way he spoke on the issue. The words, "grace under fire" came to mind. I have thought about this often. There are many unsung heroes like Larry Ward who never get much recognition. I learned a lot from Larry on that day.

Just as you witness courageous battles, humorous events, and sad times in politics, you also witness what I would call "unhappy landings" — situations where people just end up "holding the bag" for someone else's doings. These, too, remind us all of the human dimension of politics.

The concept of ministerial responsibility, whereby one person is accountable to the public through the legislature, is a good and necessary one, but its casualties sometimes seem unfair whether they are in the national or provincial political scene. It seems odd, for example, that former federal Liberal Human Resources and Development Minister Jane Stewart endured so much wrath over the "billion-dollar boondoggle" at HRDC (Human Resources Development Canada). This involved what the auditor general of Canada's report described as sloppy paperwork, careless spending and vague job creation figures all of which contributed to alleged massive mismanagement of its one billion dollar jobs grants program, resulting in some improper payments, inadequate oversight of spending and the like. She inherited the whole mess from her predecessors, including Pierre Pettigrew. No one ever seemed to point out that he had been responsible during a good part of the period when all of the alleged infractions happened. He left. She stepped in. She was left "holding the bag."

There are times when the whole truth is just not revealed. I can't think of many people more dedicated or honest than Doreen Hamilton, a former Regina Wascana Plains MLA. Doreen's popularity and reputation allowed her to win a tough seat for the NDP on more than one occasion. She served in cabinet for a time, but ultimately was dropped as a result of events at the Saskatchewan Liquor and Gaming Authority, an agency for which she was the minister responsible.

The events in question involved the firing of an SLGA employee, a former RCMP officer, for notifying police about alleged fraud at Saskatchewan Indian Gaming Authority. This firing was controversial, since people encourage and support the concept of "whistle-blowing". The firing was not the doing of Doreen, but of various public servants, with the full knowledge and consent of specific politicians. She was left to defend the indefensible, since she was the minister in charge when the questions arose. Ultimately, when the story got hot, Doreen took responsibility and left cabinet. She went on from this dark moment, in typical "Doreen" fashion, to serve her constituents and the government very well.

Similarly, the dropping of Saskatoon's Judy Junor from cabinet, which did not arise from any particular issue or event but, simply, as a result of the premier's wish to reduce the size of cabinet, did not seem to break her stride. She continued to hold her head up, attend community events and serve her constituents.

To me, the examples of Doreen and Judy serve to illustrate that we are elected as MLAs to serve our constituents. That is our priority, and our most important job. In the final analysis, it is not the "power plays" that make or break a politician's reputation.

No recounting of the characters in the legislature throughout the 1990s, though, would be complete without a mention of the colourful and irrepressible Pat Lorje, three-time member for the constituency of Saskatoon Wildwood.

If I am someone who speaks my mind, Pat blared hers. She served with distinction as a member of Saskatoon City Council from 1979 to 1991, and the Legislature from 1991 to 2003. A political career spanning twenty-four years with no electoral defeats is quite impressive. And, in 2006, Pat was once again elected to Saskatoon City Council.

Given Pat's sometimes controversial role as a politician, some have dismissed her as some kind of gadfly or maverick. They should look more closely. Gadflies do not last more than three decades in politics. Pat is, in fact, a highly intelligent, astute, incredibly hardworking person. She served her constituents well. She made meaningful contributions during her service as a cabinet minister. Her cabinet post unfortunately came to an end too soon over a relatively minor incident. She gently touched an employee while admonishing her, an incident that was deemed inappropriate but which insiders knew was blown ridiculously out of proportion.

Pat was one of those "take it or leave it" people who "told it as she saw it". One of those people you either love or hate. She had plenty of fans, and lots of detractors. Although I think Pat sometimes spoke too soon, her dedication to her constituents and the public interest was very real, as anyone who locked horns with her would testify. I sometimes had fiery arguments with Pat, but life at the legislature wasn't nearly as exciting after her 2003 retirement from provincial politics.

Many people crossed my political trails whose individuality, humanity and courage I will not forget. What made them choose politics as a career I can only speculate, but one common thread that they all shared was that they wanted to make a positive difference in other peoples' lives. I can vouch for those I've mentioned here; they really did want to make our province, and the world, a better place.

The Perspective of Legacy

THE MOST GRATIFYING PART OF SERVING IN POLITICS is looking at programs or projects operating successfully, which you have played some small part to bring about.

Shortly after Roy Romanow was defeated in the 1982 provincial election, the end of the first stage of his political career, I asked him what his proudest accomplishment as an MLA and cabinet minister had been. It seemed likely to me that since Roy was Attorney General for eleven years his answer would be the creation of the Human Rights Commission, Legal Aid, constitutional change or some such lofty and law-related matter. I was surprised when he said that he was most proud of the creation of the Meewasin Valley Authority (MVA).

The MVA had been created in the latter part of the last Blakeney government to protect and develop the beauty of the South Saskatchewan river valley in Saskatoon and the surrounding rural municipality of Corman Park, in the same way that the Wascana Centre Authority does this for the large park surrounding the legislative building in Regina.

Roy said that he felt good when he saw the beauty enhanced by the MVA in his home community of Saskatoon. By the time our conversation occurred in 1982, virtually everyone agreed.

That had not always been the case. When the MVA legislation was put to the legislature in 1979 much controversy arose. The basic plan was sound. But the government mishandled some aspects of the Bill, including a provision that resulted in caveats being placed on all the land owned in the conservation and buffer zones in the Meewasin Valley, a sixty-kilometre stretch of land along the South Saskatchewan River. These were placed on legal descriptions, which took up twelve full pages in the regulations and represented thousands of individual land holdings. This, not surprisingly, upset land owners. Some called Roy and Premier Allan Blakeney "communists", and it was said that the NDP government wanted to take over people's land, the usual claptrap trotted out by the right wing. They told people something to the effect that they wouldn't be able to "plant a flower" in the large control zone without government approval.

I doubted that either Roy or Allan Blakeney had time to approve everyone's yardwork so, even as a resident of the area, I wasn't too worried. Some Conservatives in Riversdale, however, saw their opportunity to "get Roy", so they began to organize a public meeting of the Riversdale Community Association to condemn this dastardly plan of our MLA, and the minister in charge, Roy Romanow.

Not to be undone by the competition, Myrna Hewitt, Mike Finley and I, along with others, decided we would attend the party as well, along with a few of our friends. We set about contacting people in Riversdale. Our message was, "Roy needs our help." He was trying to do something good and worthwhile, and it was unfair for people to raise fear and engage in over-the-top name calling motivated by political deception.

Sometimes, people manage to shine. I was happy the night of the public meeting to see hundreds of people show up to defeat the motion condemning the MVA. After the vote, the right-wingers stormed out of the meeting angrily. They had lost that battle, although they were able to celebrate on election night, 1982, when they finally managed to defeat Roy at the polls. Although the loss must have been very hard for Roy, the main comment I recall him making was quite witty: "I have retired from politics, with the full consent of the voters of Saskatoon Riversdale."

Roy did have a sense of humour and a quick mind. A few years later, when he became provincial NDP leader, Premier Grant Devine referred to him as "a spineless political playboy." Roy's response: "That was just a lucky guess!"

I could relate to Roy's pride in the MVA looking back at developments I had a hand in. It is not always the major legislative changes or the sweeping reforms that bring great satisfaction. When I was the minister of Health, we opened a new health centre in La Ronge, replacing the old hospital. There had been controversy over pediatric beds, as some believed the number planned for could not accommodate the number of children who were routinely hospitalized in La Ronge. While I was concerned with the controversy then, later, as Finance minister, I saw that we embarked on a program to spend millions of dollars over several years to improve water quality in northern communities. Soon an important connection was to be made. It occurred one day, when the cabinet was meeting in La Ronge and I was touring some economy-related sites. Health Minister John Nilson told me about his visit to the La Ronge Health Centre. "Remember the controversy about the number of kids' beds?" John asked. "Today, there are no kids in the hospital. Most of the problems they used to come in for were stomach problems from dirty water, and the water is now being cleaned up."

The connection was not lost on me, as it graphically brought home the importance of preventive health, and I was glad we had made the decision to do more to clean up the water system. It also made me feel good to know that I had played some small part in this decision and that the children in northern communities were healthier because of it.

I also felt proud to see advancements such as the impressive new Kinesiology Building and Chemistry Building addition at the University of Saskatchewan in Saskatoon, and the Physical Activity Centre and other new buildings at the University of Regina. I had been directly involved in finding the money to move the projects along.

Another project in which I had a hand was one of the major initiatives of the 2001 budget called "community net" which took high-speed internet to most communities of over 200 people, and which made Saskatchewan the most "wired" place on earth. This investment made me feel that I had a part in accomplishing a major communications advance for Saskatchewan people. Don't get me wrong — it wasn't my money. It was the taxpayers' money. But, it is always satisfying to see that it has been put to good use. Just as the Meewasin Valley Authority was something Roy felt good about, cleaner water, schools and university buildings were important accomplishments for me. Seeing the results of such progressive teamwork, in many cases, made politics seem very worthwhile.

Travel Bumps and Surprises

POLITICS IN A FAR-FLUNG PROVINCE CAN BE very hectic and tiring. The meetings, briefings, media scrums, frenzied planning, and intense travel can take their toll. On many occasions, I travelled from Regina to Saskatoon and back again twice in one day, in order to attend morning and evening events in Saskatoon, and the legislature in Regina. I remember once, as minister of Health, I started my day in Regina. Then, I went to some event in Swift Current, came back to Regina to answer questions in the legislature, then went to speak in Moose Jaw, then over to a public meeting in Yorkton, after which I flew to Saskatoon. This was Regina-Swift Current-Regina-Moose Jaw-Yorkton-Saskatoon, all in one eighteen hour working day. (Perhaps an answer to those who wonder why you fly!) Each stop involved speaking, and answering tough media questions or reporting to members of the public.

Arriving back in Saskatoon after midnight, I was exhausted. I had to get up at 6:00 AM in order to be able to drive to North Battleford by 8:00 AM to speak to a meeting of the

Saskatchewan Ambulance Association. Then I hit a bureaucratic bump. Even though I needed a car to drive home from the Saskatoon Airport, and to drive on to North Battleford, after four or five hours sleep, government officials refused to leave a car available for me at the airport. Although this had sensibly been done in the past when cabinet ministers arriving after midnight needed to drive somewhere, someone in the bureaucracy had since determined that this was a "special privilege" and should not be expected. God forbid that politicians should be provided with a car at an airport after hours, in order to meet their job responsibilities.

I was furious. There I was, sent all over the damn province in one day, back to Saskatoon after midnight, expected to get a few hours sleep, then drive myself to the Battlefords while the civil service slept in their beds. And to top it off someone thought it was some kind of "perk" to provide me with transportation after midnight that I might need after less than six hours sleep.

But the story doesn't end there. I had been told before I left for Saskatoon that I would need to summon a taxi from the airport to take me downtown, where I could find a car, with keys in it at the service station that served government cars in Saskatoon. I could then take that car home and use it to drive to North Battleford in the morning.

Doing as told, I called a cab and took it to downtown Saskatoon. There was no car with keys as promised. This was not just unfortunate; it was totally aggravating, so I did the only thing I could do. I took the cab home, got into bed and dutifully drove off to North Battleford in my rusty 1986

Grand Am the next morning. It was Saturday, by the way, a real weekend treat.

At that moment, I felt really quite abused by the system. On Monday morning, I called Brian Hansen at the Saskatoon Cabinet Office and Gary Aldridge, Premier Romanow's Chief of Staff. I vigorously complained to them, not about the fact that I was expected to attend to six cities in twenty-four hours, but that the government felt that asking for some travel accommodation to do my job was inappropriate. From what I could tell, everyone denied having had anything to do with the formulation of this new rule, and it soon disappeared.

I never did find who in the bureaucracy decided I couldn't have a car left at the airport. Whoever it was didn't take the trouble to find me in order to let me know. But then again, there are those who couldn't always find me no matter how hard they claimed to be looking. SaskPower, for example, could not locate me for twenty years to pay me some money they owed me.

Somehow, around 1985, they tried to send me an interest cheque on some SaskPower bonds I owned. I'd moved, and the cheque was apparently returned to them. Twenty years later, in 2005, they published a list of "lost" people entitled to some money. If only they could be found! Officials explained how they'd searched high and low for these people, but couldn't find them, so they were appealing to the public for help.

There I was on their website! How many "Eric Cline"s are there in Saskatchewan? There are two to my knowledge. Anyway, people started phoning my office to tell me I was on the missing persons list. I phoned SaskPower and told them I was alive and well, was a fourteen-year MLA, a cabinet minister on the board of their holding company, in the phone book, one of their customers (who incidentally received a bill from them each and every month), frequently in the media (radio, TV, newspaper, internet). I explained that the SaskPower vice-president of Finance was my former deputy minister of Finance, and I had lived next door to him for twelve years. And, finally, I told them that I was a long-time friend of the president of SaskPower. I apologized for keeping such a low profile all these years, thanked them for publishing my name on their website, and they sent me my money.

As much as political life can be hectic and frustrating, it can also be full of surprises and you must be prepared for the unexpected. Certainly, a politician should expect to be asked to get up and make a speech at an event, or at least say a few words. It took me a while to get used to this, even though I had been a practicing lawyer for quite a while.

"Legal" speaking and public or political speaking are completely different. Legal presentations are often highly technical and uninteresting to non-lawyers. Public and political presentations must be done differently, and in a more engaging way.

I learned early on to be prepared for the unexpected. Certainly, I learned to get up and speak briefly on various subjects when I happened to be at a meeting where someone asked me to do so. On one occasion, I attended a banquet being held by the Canadian Nuclear Association in Saskatoon. I had been invited to join them, which I was happy to do. The legislature was in session, so I had to drive from Regina to Saskatoon for the event. It was held in the ballroom of a local hotel and about three or four hundred people were there.

I saw some people I knew, so asked if I could join them for supper, which was fine with them. After supper, while I was sitting enjoying a drink and minding my own business, the master of ceremonies went to the microphone. "Now," he said, "to introduce our guest speaker, I would like to call upon local MLA Eric Cline."

Well, I would have been happy to introduce the guest speaker. The only problem was that nobody told me I was to introduce the guest speaker. Worse, I didn't know that much about the guest speaker. It is one thing to be prepared for the unexpected, but it is quite another to prepare, on the spot, a brief introductory speech for someone you hardly know.

As I walked to the podium, I thought: "I can't get up and say no one has asked me to do this. It would make both me and the organizers look stupid and create certain tension for the guest speaker herself. I have to say something." So, when I arrived at the podium, I faced the audience and said:

I am very pleased to be here to introduce our guest speaker for this evening. I do not intend to say very much about the qualifications and accomplishments of our guest speaker. She is well known to you. And, besides, if I embarked upon a description of the accomplishments of our guest speaker, the list is so long that it would take too long to recite, and I would be intruding upon the time of our guest speaker, which would be wrong; because, you have, after all, come to listen to her — not to listen to me and (at this point I launched into a short speech about the importance of friendly relations between Canada and the United States, since I knew the guest speaker was a former governor of the state of Washington.) So, please, join me in welcoming our guest speaker.

At this point, the guest speaker, a charming woman in her sixties, approached the podium. She looked at me. She faced the audience. She said: "I have been introduced many times, in many parts of the world. And I have never been introduced . . . as warmly and graciously as I just was."

Hmm, I thought. Politics is very interesting. You can get up and make a speech on any topic, introduce people, even if you know very little about them, and be praised for it, while other times you can work and plan on making a profound speech that falls on deaf ears! And what makes politics so surprising is that you just never know how people are going to respond, whether they are strangers or your own colleagues.

You never know when the public will be interested in you, and you never know what they will do with that interest. One day, while in Regina, I was talking to my constituency assistant Donna Rederburg on the phone.

"And, oh," she said. "You're in a painting at the Mendel Art Gallery."

This was news to me. "Why would I be in a painting at the Mendel Art Gallery?"

"I don't know," Donna said. "Delores Galeschuk was down there and saw you in a painting. Roy Romanow is in it too."

Intrigued, I thought I had better check this out when I got back home to Saskatoon. Once home, I went down to the gallery and, sure enough, there was a very large and beautifully painted work by Prince Albert artist Myles McDonald. I was in it, dressed as a court jester, hanging onto the side of a castle. Roy Romanow, Pierre Trudeau, Jackie Onassis, Jean Chretien and all kinds of other people were in it, too. I think Roy was a puppet, with the strings being pulled by someone else, either Trudeau or Chretien. I phoned Roy and told him he was in a painting at the Mendel Art Gallery.

"Why would I be in a painting at the Mendel Art Gallery?" he asked.

"How should I know?" I responded.

You might think that being immortalized in a painting would bring a more profound response, but just as politics can be surprising, it can also be bewildering at times.

The Portfolio Dance

THE ONE COMMITMENT YOU MUST ALWAYS MAKE in politics is that you must also be prepared to work with colleagues, and abide by the decision of the majority. There can be no surprise to anyone in your "on-the-record" response. I have already described how the introduction of no fault insurance in 1994 was a difficult issue for me, since I was a litigation lawyer. The NDP caucus, however, and most of the public, were in favour. It would keep insurance rates lower than the soaring rates in other parts of Canada and it would promote rehabilitation of accident victims by shifting money away from lawyers, courts and awards for "pain and suffering" toward medical and other services and income support needed by badly-injured people.

I went along with the majority on the issue and "no fault" insurance came into existence. Subsequently, the Saskatchewan Government Insurance agency inadvertently released a memorandum I wrote in the early stages of the no fault discussion within government. It became public knowledge, reported by the media, that I had resisted the no fault plan. Selective source quotes are the bane of all politicians as they can create misinformation and require damage control.

So, when I became minister of Justice and Attorney General in February 2003 after the resignation of Chris Axworthy, the legal profession justifiably felt there might be hope for change to the no fault legislation. By then, however, the no fault plan had been in place for eight years. I had watched it in practice, and had concluded that it was, in fact, a better plan than the old system. So, I wasn't surprised when the Canadian Bar Association (Saskatchewan) and the Law Society of Saskatchewan came to see me to discuss the matter. While, as a lawyer, I did understand their motivation, I told them that I felt the evidence showed people received better compensation under the new plan. I firmly believe that to be the case. I also knew that any time a minister changes a portfolio, the lobby groups will appear and I was ready.

My move to the Justice portfolio arose largely because, when Chris Axworthy resigned, there was no lawyer within government available to take the job other than John Nilson, but he had already been minister of Justice and was doing a good job as Health minister. Thus, in February 2003, I was moved from the Finance portfolio, which I had held since 1997. At the same time as I became minister of Justice, I became minister of Industry and Resources. This portfolio was actually the combination of two former departments, namely the Department of Economic Development and the Department of Energy and Mines. Thus, I was now responsible for what had, up until recently, been done by three separate ministers. Whether I was ready or not, I had the responsibility.

During my previous five and one-half years as minister of Finance, I enjoyed my job immensely. It is great to get up every morning eager to go to work. Finance is the "central agency" of government, and, as Finance minister, you have an opportunity to see how each part of the government functions. Moreover, working with the officials of the department was a pleasure. They were professional, non-partisan and competent. Bill Jones was succeeded by Paul Boothe and then Ron Styles as deputy minister. Each, in turn, and their officials, were invaluable in helping me carry out my duties.

The finance job was demanding and took very long hours, but I liked it, and wanted to do it for the rest of my political career. I was happy when the new Premier, Lorne Calvert, kept me on when he assumed the premier's chair in February 2001. It is unrealistic, however, to expect to stay in one place indefinitely. I had already served longer than anyone on the job in the last forty years, and longer than all of the other federal-provincial-territorial Finance ministers except one. So, it was natural that my term would have to end. And, with the resignation of Justice Minister Chris Axworthy in February 2003, it became inevitable.

It is one of the popular misconceptions that "most politicians are lawyers." When I hear this, I ask the person saying it how many of the fifty-eight MLAs in Saskatchewan they think are lawyers. Usually, they answer "Twenty or so." I then tell them that, when I left politics in 2007, there were four lawyers in the legislature, namely myself, John Nilson, QC, Frank Quennell, QC and Don Morgan, QC. That made for three lawyers in government, one in opposition. The most I have seen at one time in the assembly is seven, and several of them were not practicing lawyers. The situation remained the same after the election of the Saskatchewan Party government.

In any event, in February 2003 there were only two of us in government. Jack Hillson had left the NDP-Liberal coalition, and he wasn't coming back. If you wanted a lawyer as minister of Justice, which had always been the tradition in Saskatchewan, there was only one choice, namely me.

I had tried to convince Chris Axworthy to remain in the legislature and in cabinet. After serving from 1988 to 1999 as an NDP Member of Parliament, Chris had joined the Romanow government as minister of Justice and Attorney General. Bright, charming and articulate, Chris was a good addition to government, and handily won elections in the Saskatoon-Fairview seat vacated by the respected veteran of legal and political affairs, Bob Mitchell, QC.

One of the reasons Chris ran provincially was to be in government. He was tired of being only an opposition complainer. I think, too, he saw the opportunity to take over the leadership from Roy Romanow and to become premier. After Roy Romanow stepped down, Chris ran against Lorne Calvert for the provincial NDP leadership and finished second.

Observing Chris in cabinet, it appeared to me that he never got over losing the all-membership leadership vote to Lorne Calvert. I knew he was unhappy in his role as a cabinet minister, and feared that he would leave, which would be a loss to government and, I knew, also meant I would likely have to leave the Finance portfolio I loved and move to Justice.

I also felt that Chris should examine the opportunity he had to play a constructive role as an agent of change. After a public event in Saskatoon one summer afternoon in 2002, I invited Chris for a beer at a local tavern. I told him that I sensed what he was thinking, but I felt he was missing a big opportunity to make a difference. I told him many lawyers would give their eye teeth to have the opportunity to be minister of Justice and pursue reforms and programs they believed in. I said that I'd had the opportunity to radically change the taxation system and, with colleagues, work on welfare reform, bring in a highways plan, and new economic incentives for oil and gas and mining. I said that if I left politics tomorrow, I would be okay with it in the sense that I would feel that I had made some positive contribution, that I had made a difference.

"What have you done?" I asked. "What have you accomplished? Don't you think you should stay and make change?"

Chris told me that he thought I was right, and he should stay and achieve worthwhile change. (God knows we have problems in the justice system in Saskatchewan that arise out of poverty.) There is much to be done. But, in the end, Chris' unhappiness with the result of the leadership vote led him to leave within six months of our conversation. With his departure, I had new responsibilities. I was responsible for the two main portfolios of Industry and Resources, and Justice and Attorney General, and both involved issues that were of keen interest to the media and the voting public alike.

A Brief Stop at Justice and Crime

"CHANGE IS AS GOOD AS A REST," the old cliché says. Much to my surprise, it seemed to be true, as I felt reinvigorated and energized by the responsibilities of my new portfolio.

I had never seen myself as minister of Industry and Resources, but I felt that, if I could contribute to the growth of the economy and jobs, it would be very satisfying. In fact, I took to it immediately, and began to work with business people and industries throughout the province.

The tasks assigned to me were somewhat daunting. In addition to Industry and Resources (two departments combined into one) I was minister of Justice and Attorney General and minister responsible for the then controversial Information Services Corporation. Given the scope of these departments, I was relieved to find competent leadership at the top of each of these agencies in the expertise of Larry Spannier (Industry and Resources), Doug Moen, QC (Justice) and Mark MacLeod (ISC). Our first challenge was that, in tune with my plan to have major themes and objectives for the next term, I had to determine what my priorities should be, and to convince my government colleagues that these were, indeed, priorities for government as well.

I would have my hands full with the two main portfolios of Industry and Resources, on the one hand, and Justice and Attorney General on the other, but I was determined I would not short-change either of these departments. Each deserved a full time minister, and I would give each my full attention even though I always had the sense that I would be Justice minister for an interim period. At this time, I also became vice-chair of the Treasury Board which, as of February 2003, was chaired by the new Finance minister, Jim Melenchuk, my former Liberal seatmate. Everyone agreed that Jim had done a great job as minister of Learning. He had been a very capable family physician and was regarded as a very able cabinet minister. It was common knowledge that Jim's contributions to cabinet discussions were always well informed and well prepared. I was glad to see Jim in the Finance portfolio, and sorry that he only had the opportunity to present one budget before being narrowly defeated in the 2003 election. I welcomed continued involvement on the Treasury Board, given my role as chair from 1997 to 2003.

The real challenge in my change in portfolios came with the societal perception and expectation of the Justice department. The Justice minister is highly visible as media attention is constant. It is no secret that Saskatchewan has a high crime rate and a high incarceration rate. Anyone who becomes Justice minister has to deal with these realities. The problems are complex, and cannot be solved by the Justice Department alone, but it is where the public looks first in addressing these concerns. The crime statistics in Saskatchewan are a reflection of inequality and poverty that results from historical treatment and dislocation of the aboriginal community. A further complicating factor is that the aboriginal community is going through a transition from rural and reserve life to, increasingly, urban life. The problems generated by such conditions are immediate and real; the solutions are not.

If the crime problem is to be solved, and I think eventually it can be, it will not be solved primarily in the justice system. It will be solved by education, job creation and adequate housing, among other things. Certainly, there are interventions that police, prosecutors and other Justice officials can undertake to resolve the crime problem, including restorative justice programs and targeted anti-crime programs such as those currently undertaken by the police and the Justice Department. In a positive sense, Saskatchewan is well ahead of other jurisdictions in these kinds of programs. But, the problems are more extensive in Saskatchewan than in most other places.

The fact remains that the police, prosecutors and courts deal with the symptoms of wider societal problems. In order to deal with crime, we need to deal with its causes. It was a priority of the NDP government to put more resources into programs for community schools in areas of high poverty. Ultimately, education, training, and jobs will be some of the keys to involving every sector of society equally in our economy and community. While Finance minister, I had worked with Jim Melenchuk to devote much more funding to education programs like community schools and special education. Still, more remains to be done to find long-term solutions. Investment in training for employment is crucial, and is a major focus of government.

I made it my priority as minister of Justice to ensure that alternate forms of dealing with crime such as mediation/ diversion and restorative justice were promoted as much as possible. I wanted to make sure that justice was seen to be done in resolving unanswered questions surrounding the tragic and complex 1990 death of teenager Neil Stonechild in Saskatoon. In addition, with the Commission on Aboriginal Justice started by Chris Axworthy underway, my hope was that, together, these two inquiries would help us lead the justice system to relate more effectively to the aboriginal community and bring public awareness to events that affected them.

The overriding goal, however, remains to fashion an economy and a society in which there is the kind of personal and economic opportunity and participation that engages all communities equally.

In my relatively brief tenure as Justice minister I initiated some of Saskatchewan's most publicized and important justice inquiries including those concerning the death of Neil Stonechild and the wrongful conviction of David Milgaard. These inquiries have generated reams of transcripts and the stories have produced books in their own right. As emotional as these public inquiries were, it is hoped that they demonstrated that governments can act and can listen. And, as the media coverage of these events exposed, the complexity and intricacy of how justice is both perceived and enacted is tortuous and often perplexing.

There were many difficult moments of heartache and sadness during my time as Justice minister. Whether coming to terms with police reform, facing the media on sensationalized lawsuits, or authorizing the prosecution of David

Ahenakew, former national Chief of the Assembly of First Nations, for a hate crime, the clash of law and justice is complex. As an elected politician, I had to serve the people; as minister of Justice, I had to promote the rule of law. It often required every ounce of my energy and conviction to see my duties through. One can only hope that the long-term gains of these actions ultimately contribute to positive change in Saskatchewan's future.

Resource Power

AS MINISTER OF INDUSTRY AND RESOURCES, my priority and main responsibility would, of course, be to encourage economic development and stimulate job creation. This is a major concern for any government and essential to the well being of any province.

Starting in the early 1990s, under the leadership of Dwain Lingenfelter, the Department of Economic Development, as it then was, had developed a fairly good economic development strategy entitled "Partnership For Prosperity". The strategy identified key sectors for economic growth, steps that needed to be taken to achieve the growth, targets to be met and a timetable and accountability system to ensure government got the job done. It was regularly updated under the Romanow and Calvert administrations.

As Industry and Resources minister, I worked with Premier Calvert to host the Centennial Economic Summit in January 2005. This Summit brought together representatives of all parts of Saskatchewan society. Everyone saw it as a highly successful meeting because there was a very frank exchange of views. It was the first major event hosted by the government to kick off the province's centennial year. I undertook at the end of the Summit to take what we had heard and devise a new economic action plan for Saskatchewan. With the release of the Action Plan on the Economy in the fall of 2005, that is what we did.

Earlier, as minister of Finance, I had already begun to do some work that I felt was necessary to stimulate the economy. In cooperation with Eldon Lautermilch, the minister of Energy and Mines before it was combined with Economic Development, we worked to bring about further development of both the oil and gas and mining sectors. For Eldon, who was much maligned for his role in the Spudco affair, it was appropriate vindication. The Spudco affair had dominated the political news in Saskatchewan in the late 90s. Everyone knew how the story ended after the premier responsibly conducted an internal review of the matter. In the end, the dream of a potato industry built with government support faltered when the company ran out of money and those who invested in it, including the government, were left holding the bag. While there were some significant problems in the government's enthusiasm to invest in such a project, the economic intention was above board. While the Perrins report, as the premier's internal review was known, cleared the innuendo and speculation with facts, in popular perception responsibility for the affair was placed at the feet of the minister then in charge, Eldon Lautermilch. Others were mainly responsible for the Spudco affair. Some of the key players have emerged unscathed. In politics, blame is quickly assigned, and good work seldom acknowledged. Eldon did a lot of good work as House leader, minister of Energy and Mines, minister of Economic Development and minister of Highways, among others. Yet none of his accomplishments attracted the media's interest in him as much as when the NDP government's decision to help expand the province's potato industry in the Lake Diefenbaker area blew up, while he was in charge.

Under Eldon's watch, the oil and gas sector grew considerably in the 1990s. Mining was also doing well. Eldon, along with his predecessor Doug Anguish, contributed positively to these developments. Eldon was personally responsible, along with Liberal MP Ralph Goodale, for the creation of the Petroleum Technology Research Centre, which was crucial to the development of Saskatchewan's oil resources.

Working together, Eldon and I instructed our respective departments of Energy and Mines and Finance to collaborate on initiatives to encourage more oil and gas drilling and production and more exploration, prospecting and development in the mining sector. Expedient and careful planning could only be achieved with such collaboration.

These matters are always more complex than they seem, but given the immense economic importance of natural resource development, the public demanded action. On the oil and gas side, it took a few years of discussions with the industry to identify the most effective ways to encourage more activity, and promote profitability due to a complex taxation structure. Working together, the departments involved were able to come up with a royalty and taxation system which provided that new drilling after November 1, 2002 would be subject to taxation similar to what it is in Alberta.

Again, I found myself in battles with both the political right and the left. The right wing likes to claim that there are no differences between Alberta and Saskatchewan oil and gas resources. They say the only difference is the political will, and that, from the beginning, Tommy Douglas prevented the industry from growing. Their myth concludes that if it wasn't for the CCF-NDP, Saskatchewan would be as rich as Alberta.

In fact, there are major differences between the oil and gas resources of Alberta and Saskatchewan, as any competent geologist will attest. One of the problems with Saskatchewan oil is that, of all the known reserves, only about fifteen percent is recoverable using conventional technology. The rest cannot be removed, and stays in the ground. That is why it is important to do research into ways to get Saskatchewan's oil to the surface. Work is underway at the Petroleum Technology Research Centre in Regina to do just that, thanks to the co-operation of the federal and provincial governments, the University of Regina, the Saskatchewan Research Council, and industry.

Meanwhile, the private sector is also creatively trying to get more out of the ground at sites such as Encana's project near Weyburn and Apache's at Midale, where carbon dioxide (CO_2) is injected into the ground in an effort to create more underground pressure to move oil into pools from which it can be brought to the surface.

Given the unique nature of Saskatchewan's oil reserves, it is important that these efforts continue, and that the federal and provincial governments work together to ensure that appropriate taxation and equalization treatment exists to allow innovation. The federal government has co-operated with the province in some minor ways, but much more remains to be done to treat Saskatchewan and its resources more fairly, especially given the fact that provinces such as Nova Scotia and Newfoundland and Labrador receive preferential tax treatment. Stephen Harper promised to correct this before and during the 2006 federal election, in no uncertain terms. Once he became prime minister, however, his tune changed, and Saskatchewan continued to be denied the same concessions that other provinces receive.

Unlike Saskatchewan, Alberta has a history of having a more abundant reserve of light sweet crude, which is easier to develop and more profitable. The real petroleum industry difference between Alberta and Saskatchewan, however, is the fact that Alberta's natural gas resource is so many times larger than Saskatchewan's. People don't often realize that the big money being made and huge surpluses accumulated by Alberta these days come mostly from natural gas. Oil sands now play an increasing role as well. While the conventional oil resource of Alberta is about four times that of Saskatchewan, their gas reserves are at least twenty-five times as big as Saskatchewan's. In fact, while Saskatchewan is number two in Canada for oil, we actually are number three for gas, since British Columbia also has more natural gas resources than Saskatchewan.

None of this information should distract us from doing all we can to develop our heavier crude oil and our smaller gas resources. The industry doubled in size under the Romanow and Calvert governments, and the incentives are there for that growth to continue. While right-wing critics spent their time complaining that the NDP wouldn't develop oil and gas, we simply kept moving forward doing just that.

Another myth trotted out by Conservative politicians and their supporters is that Saskatchewan has some huge tar sand resource similar to Alberta's. They say that the only reason it isn't developed is that the government consciously prevents it from happening. They say that the tar sands do not end at the Alberta-Saskatchewan border and that they are here waiting to be worked. What they do not say is that although the tar sands don't end at the border, they go very deep into the earth. Any qualified geologist could tell them that no one has yet been able to find tar sands in Saskatchewan at a depth or quantity that would make production profitable. The politics of Saskatchewan have nothing to do with the matter; it is a question of geology. Now that the price of oil has skyrocketed, there may be enough financial incentive to successfully exploit tar sands on the Saskatchewan side, and this is being actively explored. The Saskatchewan Party has suggested for years that they would quickly develop Saskatchewan tar sands with the NDP out of the way. Now that they are in power, they have the opportunity to do so, if they're not too busy building the nuclear reactors they also implied would surely spring up under their tenure.

The importance of geology cannot be emphasized enough when it comes to natural resource development. It is geology that dictates that Saskatchewan is the largest potash producer in the world and the largest uranium producer in the world. Alberta does not produce potash or uranium. It makes about as much sense to rant about Alberta having more gas and oil development than Saskatchewan as it does to rant about Saskatchewan having more potash and uranium development than Alberta. Does the Alberta government have no interest in the development of their uranium? Of course not. It is simply not developed because geology makes it expensive and difficult to develop on the Alberta side.

When establishing stubborn and impractical political views, it is always important to maintain a balance. In that sense, it is fortunate that the cranky views of the right on resource development and gas are balanced off by cranky views on the left.

The left wing believes that the oil and gas industry will develop regardless of the royalty and tax structure. They propose that the government has no business creating a receptive environment for private sector investment. They suggest that if the industry doesn't develop itself, maybe we're better to leave oil and gas in the ground anyway. This is the "non-development" development strategy. Ironically people whose salaries come from the public sector, including universities, often espouse this view. I often wonder where they think the taxes come from to pay for the public services and institutions we all rely upon and in which some of them work. Certainly the public sector can and does contribute to a healthy economy, but so does the private sector. You need both.

As minister of Industry and Resources I refused to accept the myopic strategy of those who said we should leave the oil and gas in the ground. I knew we had to develop it responsibly because it meant jobs and economic spin-offs that ultimately build a stronger economy in Saskatchewan. The more than 24,000 jobs provided by the oil and gas sector in Saskatchewan represent 24,000 families, 24,000 homes and 24,000 opportunities for young people. Moreover, with the demographic challenges that Saskatchewan faces and the need to involve everyone in the economy, we simply cannot afford to ignore the continued opportunities for economic and employment growth.

When Premier Calvert took office in February 2001, he made it clear that it was a high priority for him to have economic progress. Many times he said that as a social democrat he believes in social progress and that we can't have social progress without economic progress. Changes in oil and gas, mining and other sectors do not occur without the full backing of the premier.

While oil and gas is now the largest part of Saskatchewan's economy, mining, along with manufacturing, rivals agriculture for second place, and is also a very important contributor to our economy. It was therefore also important in the fall of 2002 to effect changes in the development of Saskatchewan mining. These changes also came in the form of a package of incentives to encourage more exploration and prospecting for mineral resources. Because mining is big business in Saskatchewan and provides a lot of jobs, and because Saskatchewan is a world recognized mining jurisdiction, long-term vision is required to ensure the sector continues to thrive and grow.

Mining development requires even longer-term thinking than oil and gas. While changes on the oil and gas side can mean more drilling in the next week, mines cost hundreds of millions or even billions of dollars. It takes years of exploration and analyses before a mining company can decide to commit to that kind of investment. Oil and gas companies expect to drill and have some "dry holes". Mining companies can't afford to have any "dry mines". They cost too much money.

For example, a diamond mine in Saskatchewan would involve hundreds of millions of exploration expenditure and could cost in the neighbourhood of a billion dollars to build. Years of exploratory work are required to ensure that, if a mine is built, it will produce enough diamonds to pay for that kind of expenditure, plus return a profit. In addition, onerous regulatory approval processes at the provincial and federal levels have to be met for a mine to proceed, and this can take years, especially if the federal government is involved.

The Cigar Lake uranium mine, for example, was first explored in the early 1980s. Ongoing exploration, investment decisions, and regulatory processes combined to create a twenty-four year delay from initial exploration to approval of the mine, with construction and production to follow that. Therefore, when a politician is formulating policy for the mining sector, he or she is looking far ahead.

In my case, I am aware that some of the things we did in the early 2000s will lead to major developments for many years to come. Significant changes take time and patience. It is gratifying for me to think that our work will benefit people in the future. This does not mean to suggest that people do not benefit right away at the exploratory stage. In fact, the hundreds of millions of dollars being spent annually on exploration activities in Saskatchewan result in hundreds of jobs involving prospectors, geologists, engineers, contractors, labourers, tradespeople and others. The rewards begin now and grow in the future.

I have discussed oil and gas and mining at some length because these are very large sectors, and because much of my work involved changes in these areas. My intention was not to take away from the importance of other parts of the Saskatchewan economy. Forestry, agriculture, manufacturing, advanced technology, and biotechnology are other important and growing sectors of our economy and contribute to our increasing standard of living. But from a political viewpoint, it is important to realize that those elected to government must have a far-sighted approach. Although they may be defeated in the next election, good work resulting from their long-term vision can continue for decades.

Sometimes people expressed disagreement with me over what they saw as my emphasis on promoting Saskatchewan's resource development. They saw this as reflecting an emphasis on the "old" resource-based economy as opposed to the "new" (innovation and technology) economy. I believe this is a false distinction.

Firstly, it only makes sense to rely on your strengths. If you have resources, you should take advantage of them. When you develop industries like oil and gas, mining and forestry, you will build the "new" economy at the same time. Profitable "old" economy industries need innovation and technology to be competitive. For example, modern sawmills employ computers to determine how the logs should be cut. Mines require unique mechanical engineering solutions, and sometimes robotics, as well as chemical engineering expertise. The oil sector requires new chemical and other advanced methods to improve oil production.

If you build on the province's natural resource strength, you will continue to build the "new" economy of technology and innovation. The two are not distinct, but complementary. For example, Saskatoon has a world-class precision machining industry because of the demands of Saskatchewan's mining sector. At Prairie Machine, world-class mining machines worth approximately seven to eight million dollars are now manufactured for use in our potash mines. All three major potash companies in Saskatchewan have purchased these machines, manufactured in Saskatoon. We should be very proud of Murray Popplewell and his staff for producing these right here in our province. Many people are actually unaware of the level of manufacturing expertise we have in Saskatchewan. Startco Engineering in Saskatoon, which incidentally also produces the "Eye on the Hog" device used in international competitive curling, manufactures the sophisticated electrical system used to power underground mining machines. There are a lot of innovators in Saskatchewan, and these particular innovative companies spring from the resource sector and are examples of older industry spawning new ones. As well, the engineering sector in Saskatchewan experienced rapid growth from the late 1990s, based largely on the booming mining sector.

Saskatchewan's resources sector is expanding but so, too, are the important advanced technology and biotechnology sectors. International Road Dynamics, Massload Technologies, Vecima and SED Systems are just a few examples of this evolution. With the opening of the synchrotron in Saskatoon and the huge agricultural biotechnology sector in Saskatoon, we can justifiably claim that Saskatoon is Canada's "Science City". With Innovation Place in Saskatoon and Regina and the new Forestry Centre in Prince Albert, along with our universities, the Saskatchewan Research Council and partners like Agriculture Canada, the National Plant Biotechnology Institute, and the Vaccine and Infectious Diseases Organization, Saskatchewan's innovation agenda will continue to grow. We will see "old" economy and "new" economy sectors providing jobs and opportunities for people in our future.

No matter what resource the government encourages, as minister you have to have a balance between the rightful expectation of the companies to make a reasonable profit on their risk and investment, and the legitimate expectation of the public for a reasonable return out of the exploitation of their non-renewable resource. It is always a balance, and that balance will be different, depending on the industry. Because of the quality of Saskatchewan's potash and uranium, royalties set by government are high. In other sectors, like sodium sulphate and coal, royalties are kept low because of the less rich nature of the resource. A key role for the minister responsible is managing a reasonable return to Saskatchewan people while keeping the incentive for companies meaningful.

Starting in 2003, I began to speak publicly about the need to upgrade the uranium yellow cake produced in Saskatchewan. Ultimately, it became part of our Action Plan on the Economy released in September 2005. Uranium processing is the most realistic additional downstream activity we can do in the uranium sector because markets are growing. Eventually, Cameco and Areva will have to increase production and they will need more processing capacity than presently exists in Ontario. Why shouldn't we pursue that opportunity here? If you mine uranium, it has to be processed, and it may as well be processed in Saskatchewan.

I wondered when I began to speak about uranium processing whether it would meet with public approval. Despite its increasingly efficient safety record, concerns about radiation and waste management had dogged uranium companies for decades. In fact, the vast majority of people approve continued development of the uranium industry, as demonstrated in the fall of 2005, when two resolutions at the NDP convention in Regina calling upon the government to reject the notion of refining uranium were soundly defeated by about eighty percent of the party members.

Times change, as does the base of knowledge we have to make informed decisions.

Today, the people of Saskatchewan have a legitimate expectation that their resources, once extracted here, will also be processed here to the extent practical. They seek opportunities for their children and grandchildren and security for the well being of their province.

Time Travel

WHILE THE WORK OF A PROVINCIAL MINISTER involves serious problem solving and planning in the office, it also affords and demands a wider viewpoint through local, national and international travel. It allows you to meet a lot of interesting and influential people, like US Vice-President Dick Cheney or Consul General Pamela Wallin, or observe first hand the quirks of your travelling colleagues. Such travel experiences can also lead to unexpected and, sometimes, amusing situations whether they be in Rosetown or Shanghai.

I like to be on time for events, but found it was often challenging when travelling with politicians. It is quite a chore to get most of them from point A to point B. For one thing, they can never stop talking and this makes it difficult to keep them moving. My wife, Pauline knows this in spades, having tried to get me from point A to point B on many occasions as I stopped to speak with C and D and E.

One memorable evening, Carol Teichrob, Judy Bradley and I were scheduled to appear as a live phone-in panel on Shaw Cable's community station in Prince Albert, at 7:00 PM.

We were the ministers of Municipal Government, Highways and Finance respectively.

Judy was already in Prince Albert. Carol and I were to be picked up at the Bessborough Hotel in Saskatoon at 5:00 PM by Eldon Lautermilch, a Prince Albert MLA. The annual provincial NDP convention was being held at the exhibition grounds in Prince Albert that year, so we were all going there following our television appearance.

Carol and I dutifully arrived on schedule to meet Eldon in the lobby of the Bessborough around 5:00 PM, each with our luggage in tow. Eldon, however, had not arrived. We waited and I was concerned when he didn't show up by around 5:30, since Prince Albert is about 145 kilometres away, and we were scheduled to be on live TV in ninety minutes, at seven o'clock. How did Eldon expect we were going to be there on time? My concern turned to annoyance when Eldon casually sauntered into the hotel about 5:30 and proceeded to wander around talking to various mining company officials who were at some event in the hotel. Although he was, at that time, minister of Energy and Mines and his conversations with them made sense, he was also late. And, he was making us late for a live TV show.

My annoyance turned to anger when I approached Eldon and reminded him that we were supposed to be at Shaw Cable at seven o'clock, and I thought we should get going to Prince Albert. Eldon, visibly perturbed that I was interrupting his conversation with someone, turned to me. "Yes, yes, I know you are a big time TV star, and I will drive you to P.A." He then continued to visit and chat.

Now I was mad, and returned to where Carol and I had been standing. I told Carol what had happened, that I couldn't understand why he was acting that way, but that if he wasn't concerned about keeping our commitments to the people in Prince Albert, I guess I wasn't either, since I didn't have to get elected in Prince Albert. Carol didn't understand Eldon's actions either, but what could she do? I stood and silently fumed, until about ten minutes before 6:00, when Eldon finally came over to us and said he was going to get the van and would bring it around to the front door so we could load our luggage and go.

After we loaded up, Eldon and I in the front seats and Carol in the back, Eldon proceeded to drive down Spadina Crescent. Meanwhile, I had decided I would say nothing more, since Prince Albert was Eldon's constituency and problem but, as usual, I could not keep my mouth shut.

"Eldon," I said. "I simply cannot understand how you know that we are supposed to be on live TV in your community in one hour and you don't give a damn about it."

It was then that a light bulb seemed to go on above Eldon's head. He looked at me, astonished. "You mean you're supposed to be on at seven o'clock tonight? I thought it was seven o'clock tomorrow morning. I thought you just wanted to be there early to get a good night's sleep!"

"No, Eldon," I said, "We are to be there at seven o'clock tonight!" Eldon apparently did care about meeting commitments in Prince Albert after all. This was apparent by the frantic look on his face. But by then it was 6:00 and we were 145 kilometres from Shaw Cable in Prince Albert. I mentioned that Judy Bradley was also to be on the show, and was already in Prince Albert, so I guessed that she would go on alone and could handle questions until Carol and I arrived and joined her in the studio.

Unbelievably, Eldon got us to the Shaw Cable station at exactly 7:00 PM. Don't ask me how, though I think that we broke the all time record to get a politician from Saskatoon to P.A. Once there, Carol and I ran into the station as the music for the live show was beginning with someone yelling: "Where the hell are they?"

We sat down in front of the cameras, but there was no Judy Bradley waiting on the set. Where was she? This question was answered later. As it turns out, Judy Bradley was standing in the lobby of the Marlborough Hotel, waiting to be picked up by the other MLA for Prince Albert, Myron Kowalsky. Myron, meanwhile, was sitting in his Prince Albert home watching TV. As he flipped through the channels, Myron came across the community station, and saw Carol and I sitting there when the light went on above his head.

"Oh, shit!" were Myron's only words as he got up to run out of his house, pick up Judy, and deliver her to the Shaw Cable station. Around twenty minutes into the show, Judy was able to join us, but not because of Myron's last minute effort. She had waited long enough at the Marlborough, and decided to take a cab.

Eldon and Myron must have normally been more organized, because they went on to be re-elected in Prince Albert in both 1999 and 2003. I'm sure, though, some of the credit should go to their campaign managers who must have kept them on track.

If it was difficult to get Eldon from point A to point B on that occasion, it was almost impossible to get Bernie Wiens from one place to another on any occasion.

The bright, talkative, gregarious and friendly (except when confronted by anti-Canadian Wheat Board farmers or when involved in water disputes on the farm) MLA from Rosetown-Biggar was notorious for being late. This had mainly to do with Bernie's propensity to speak, at length, on any given subject to any variety of audience, large or small.

One evening, Bernie and I were scheduled to attend a public meeting in his constituency at Rosetown. We were due there at 7:00 PM, and had to fly to Saskatoon from Regina, and then drive to Rosetown. A van was to be left at the airport for us in Saskatoon.

The itinerary was tight. To be in Rosetown by seven o'clock, we had to leave Saskatoon at 5:50, so we agreed to meet at the Regina airport government hangar to fly to Saskatoon at around 4:30. That would give us ample time, since the flight to Saskatoon should take about fifty minutes. I got to the hangar about 4:30. But as 4:30 turned to 5:00 and 5:00 turned to 5:15, I began to wonder what happened to Bernie and then I began to get annoyed. The best we could now do would be to get to Saskatoon by 6:00 and arrive ten minutes late for Rosetown. So, trying to plan as best I could, I asked my assistant Murray Gross to board the plane with me and wait for Bernie there. That way, when he arrived, he could just get on board and we could leave.

Around 5:30 I saw Bernie driving up in a van driven by his deputy minister, Brent Cotter, now Dean of Law at the University of Saskatchewan. I thought for sure that Bernie would hop out, run to the plane and get on, since, by now, he would know we were running late, and would surely not get to Rosetown before 7:30. The thought of people waiting for us really bothered me.

But, as usual, Bernie was oblivious to matters of time and sat chatting away with Brent Cotter in the van for several minutes. Finally, I'd had enough. I got out of the plane, walked up to the van, opened the door, and looked at Bernie.

"Do you not realize we are to be in your constituency at seven o'clock and I have been waiting for the last hour at this airport?"

Bernie's response was to look at me as if I was out of my mind. "Would you keep a civil tongue in your head?" he asked.

This made me even madder but, again, I decided it wasn't my constituency and he could take the responsibility for keeping people waiting. So I got back on the plane and waited. Finally, Bernie got on but we didn't speak for some time. After a while, Bernie broke the ice and started chatting with me. As I said, Bernie was a talkative, gregarious and friendly guy, so by this time I had cooled off and the rest of the flight went well enough.

When we got to Saskatoon, Bernie asked me if I would drive the government vehicle to Rosetown, since he'd had so many speeding tickets, likely generated by always being late. He said that if he got another point he would lose his driver's licence. So I agreed, and taking my cue from Eldon Lautermilch, I drove quickly to Rosetown. Too quickly, actually, since the RCMP pulled us over at Vanscoy and gave me a $183 ticket for speeding, which created another ten-minute delay. Given the events of the day, I wanted to blame Bernie for this, but of course I knew I was responsible for it. What added to my annoyance, though, was that he didn't offer to share the cost of the ticket. I stopped bugging him about it only when he lost his seat in the next election to Elwin Hermanson, then leader of the Saskatchewan Party. Incidentally, the residents of Rosetown, that night, were not annoyed that they had to wait on us. They expected Bernie to be late, and planned accordingly.

There was never a dull moment with Bernie around. He was missed after he left politics in 1999, with the full support of the majority of the voters in his riding, as Roy would say.

One of my more interesting travel days has to be a twenty-four hour period spent in Shanghai, China along with my deputy minister of Industry and Resources, the late Larry Spannier, Mike Monea, then head of the Petroleum Technology Research Centre in Regina, and Michelle Oussoren from my office. Larry was a great guy with a droll sense of humour, but he wasn't amused at our treatment in Shanghai, where we were part of the "Team Canada" trade mission lead by Jim Peterson, then minister of International Trade, and Prime Minister Martin, who joined up with us in Beijing.

We had been invited to a reception hosted by the Canadian Consulate in Shanghai on the evening of our arrival. Our invitations said that the reception was to begin at 7:30 PM and sometime shortly after that Larry, Mike Monea and I decided we would attend. We dutifully presented ourselves at the ballroom in the hotel where we were staying and saw that there was much food and drink available. No one was at the reception yet, because government and consular officials were not finished briefing the hundreds of business people that were with them in an adjoining ballroom. Larry, Mike and I were not expected at that briefing, so we went back to the ballroom and obtained drinks.

As we were standing there with our drinks, a man from the Canadian Consulate came running into the room. "What are you doing in here? The reception has not started. I have to ask you to leave," he said, rudely. I was shocked by this behaviour but I said nothing. Larry protested that we had been invited, and our invitations said that the reception started at 7:30 and it was past 7:30.

Nevertheless, he insisted that we leave. I turned to Mike. "I've been kicked out of better places than this," I said. This was actually a lie, since this event was taking place in a very posh hotel. Irked, we went to the hallway to wait. Then as we were standing there, another official from the Canadian Consulate came running up to us:

"What are you doing out here in the hallway? You should be in the business briefing," she said

No one, of course, actually asked us who we were. We tried to explain that we were not registered as business members of the Canadian delegation, and so were not required to be at the briefing.

"You should go in and stand at the back of that room," this woman told us.

Up to this point, I hadn't said anything to her, but at this insistence I indicated that I didn't intend to stand at the back of any room. We continued to wait in the hallway for a few minutes until the meeting room emptied and people started entering the ballroom. Although the protocol of the Canadian Consulate staff had been needling us since we arrived, we assumed that we were finally free of their meddling and could enjoy the evening. But, no.

Later that evening, one of the senior members of the Canadian diplomatic service in Shanghai began to tell me that it was not possible to mine potash in Saskatchewan because of our outrageous tax policies. I replied in no uncertain terms that he obviously did not know what he was talking about since Saskatchewan was, in fact, the largest potash producer in the world. So for him to say that you could not mine potash in Saskatchewan was patently ridiculous and, as a minister of the Crown, I did not appreciate being lectured to by employees of the Government of Canada about our province's taxation policy, since he knew nothing about the quality of the resource. (Potash companies in Saskatchewan are doing very well, thanks.)

"I can see I have annoyed you," he said.

"You're right, you have annoyed me," I said, as I departed.

I was so fed up with the ridiculous lack of diplomatic skill demonstrated by these Canadian diplomats that I felt we should advise the federal government that we were leaving the Team Canada mission. I have hosted many receptions and on some occasions people arrive a few minutes early, before the crowd has come. We would simply tell early arrivals to make themselves at home until the others arrived. What was the big deal? Did they think that we were going to drink all their beer and eat all their food? After the exchange with the senior member of the diplomatic service, I could only think that a cardinal rule in politics is never make statements in public that make you look foolish. Obviously his diplomatic skills were at an all time low.

By the next morning, I had cooled off and I realized that it was important for our business people that we continue to participate in this trade mission. The reason we were there was not to attend receptions but to promote the interests of Saskatchewan companies to the Chinese which, of course, we proceeded to do. Later, although I did not ask for one, I did receive an apology from an official of International Trade Minister Jim Peterson's office, who apparently had been advised by someone from the Canadian Consulate about the behaviour of their officials.

Despite what happened in Shanghai, we were often greatly assisted by the many dedicated and skilled members of the Canadian diplomatic service. These individuals are very able and they help Saskatchewan and the other provinces market goods and services to the world. Although the Shanghai incident should not have happened, it is not what normally happens in the Canadian diplomatic service, for which I have tremendous respect.

Although the twenty-four hour stay in Shanghai started out badly with the reception, it improved the next day as we attended various meetings to advance Saskatchewan's industries, most notably potash and uranium. After a relatively successful and harmonious day, Larry, Mike, Michelle, and I decided to go out for supper. Larry said that there was a restaurant across the street from our hotel that looked quite nice, and we all agreed we should go there.

Not too far from the entrance, and up a set of stairs, I began to think that this was no ordinary restaurant. In fact, as we were being escorted to our booth, we passed several booths that had drawn curtains. I told Larry that I felt this was not a restaurant at all, but maybe an illegal gambling den.

Larry could be quite matter-of-fact. "This is a restaurant," he said.

I had noticed that at almost every curtained-off booth, people were playing cards.

"Larry, we are in communist China, and this is an illegal gambling den," I said.

"This is a restaurant," Larry insisted.

We sat down. A waiter came and I asked for menus.

"There are no menus," the waiter stated.

This to me, was another hint that this was not a restaurant.

"If you want food, you just go to the buffet and take what you want," the waiter told us.

I asked what the cost of the food was.

"There is no cost," the waiter said.

At that point, Larry, Mike and Michelle were also beginning to feel that perhaps this was no ordinary restaurant.

"You can have the food, but you must each pay for five beer," the waiter said.

"How much is the beer?" I asked.

The waiter explained that each bottle of beer cost what was the equivalent of about two dollars. I was hungry and the buffet looked good, so I suggested that we agree to pay the approximately ten dollars for five bottles of beer and the buffet. Ten dollars wasn't bad at all.

So, we enjoyed the buffet but did not consume all our beer. As we left, a waiter came running after us pointing out that we had left some behind. We said that was fine, but they insisted on putting the unopened beer in a brown paper bag that they gave to Mike Monea. It didn't quite seem right that Saskatchewan trade delegates should be walking around with a large doggy-bag full of beer, and Mike didn't look too comfortable. As it happened, there were some professional beggars in the area, and one approached us.

"Give her the beer," Larry told Mike.

Mike gave the woman the beer, and she was extremely happy to receive this gift, but the next thing we knew, several other professional beggars instantly surrounded Mike. Of course, he didn't have any more beer to give. "Let's get out of here," Larry said to me, so it was up to Mike to negotiate his way out of that one as Larry, Michelle and I walked quickly down the street. We knew, of course, that Mike was well trained for this kind of business negotiation.

So, two good things happened while we were in Shanghai: we had some great business meetings where we were able to brag about Saskatchewan potash and uranium, and I finally got Larry to admit that he was wrong about his position that "the restaurant" was just a restaurant.

There are many other incidents where travel placed me in situations that, had I not been a politician, I would have never found myself. Representing Saskatchewan, whether in small rural communities or on the world stage, has enriched my life in many ways.

Leadership Styles

SERVING OVER FIVE YEARS IN THE ROMANOW CABINET and over six years in the Calvert cabinet provided me with a rare opportunity to observe, close up, the different leadership styles of two premiers. Both faced worries and sleepless nights occasioned by large problems and a few scandals, which they did not cause but for which they were responsible because they happened on their watch.

I quickly learned, observing Roy Romanow agonizing over tough choices to balance the budget in the early 1990s, that being premier was not a prize but a responsibility. Tackling the issues of the day, each leader was required to apply his personality strengths and decision-making skills toward solving the government's problems. As in human affairs generally, approaches vary.

Roy Romanow would not usually make a decision until he had carefully assessed all the available facts. He liked to canvass a variety of opinions before making up his mind, including those of both experts and ordinary people.

Because Romanow would sometimes avoid making a decision until after a lengthy effort to analyze the situation, some said he was indecisive. In fact, he was very decisive; he simply would not decide until all of the available evidence was in. Once Romanow made a decision, however, it was a considered decision and he rarely changed course, regardless of opposition to his plan.

Romanow tended to surround himself with advisors who also sought rigorous policy analysis in decision-making. They would brief him before cabinet meetings as to what the best outcome would be, based on the work they had done or had requisitioned from others, inside or outside of government. Thus, Roy Romanow and his staff normally had a firm view of what the result of cabinet deliberations should be, and would be, before the discussions began. Roy's leadership style was to allow widespread discussion, listen, and ultimately inform cabinet what the consensus of the group was, and what the decision would be.

Usually, the majority of cabinet agreed with Premier Romanow's view of what the consensus of the meeting was. On some occasions, Romanow accepted the majority's views even though he personally disagreed. On a few occasions, where the vast majority of the cabinet felt one way, and the premier another, he exercised the prerogative of leaders and advised cabinet that the decision would be as he believed it should be. Respect for Premier Romanow, and trust in his judgment, which routinely proved in due course to be correct, made it easier to accept his decisions. As well, most of the cabinet understood that leaders emerge for a reason. The premier is not one among equals at a cabinet table. He or she is the first minister, and entitled, on the basis of election to that position, to act accordingly.

Of course, if a premier *was* frequently at odds with colleagues, something was seriously wrong, either with the premier or his cabinet, so such disagreements were rare.

At the same time as Premier Romanow was decisive and firm in his approach, he was a supportive leader who would back the decision of any minister who did his or her homework, attended to duty and knew his or her files. Hard work and attention to detail were rewarded and reflected in cabinet assignments.

Lorne Calvert was elected leader of the Saskatchewan New Democratic Party after nine years of a Romanow government that had made many tough and unpopular decisions in order to allow the province to recover and grow. Thus, when Calvert was elected, there was a yearning for change. The party embraced Lorne Calvert in part because they saw, in his friendly, folksy and accessible manner, hope for easier times and "feel good" leadership.

In politics, perception is often more important than reality. Although he spoke to economic issues, Premier Calvert's persona was, and is, such that he could never shake the image of a folksy socialist. To some, this was a positive thing, while those seeking middle-of-the-road leadership saw Lorne as too left wing. This is not a fair assessment of him considering his governments completed personal income tax reform, implemented changes to make the oil and gas and mining sectors more competitive, and brought in the largest business tax cuts in Saskatchewan history, including abolishing the corporate capital tax. It is, however, this assessment, made by many people, which contributed to the defeat of the NDP in 2007, when middle-of-the-road and Liberal voters abandoned the provincial NDP for the Saskatchewan Party.

Lorne Calvert deserves credit for a government that left the province in very good fiscal and economic shape when Brad Wall was elected in 2007. He also deserves credit for the election victory of 2003, when he defied the media and the pundits and won a majority government. Calvert must also, and he would undoubtedly be the first to admit it, take his share of responsibility for the 2007 defeat. That responsibility can be shared by many, of course, including me, and the defeat certainly is also attributable to the reality that the NDP had been around twice as long as governments normally last.

If the party and some of the public wanted a different leadership style when Lorne Calvert took over from Roy Romanow, they got it. If Roy sometimes took too long to make decisions while matters were reviewed and analyzed, Lorne regarded too much time spent researching topics before decisions could be made as "paralysis by analysis". He wanted decisions made and solutions found more quickly. This sometimes led to quick and inspired decisions, which provided relief to people or the end of a political problem. Other times, it led to decisions that went unnoticed because there was no lead-up or preparation for them, or that failed for the same reasons.

One decision that was made quickly on the basis of a "gut" feeling was that Saskatchewan people would pay the lowest cost for utilities (heat, electrical, telephone and insurance) in Canada. The premier implemented it in 2003 with little study, and delivered it to Saskatchewan consumers from 2003 until Premier Wall dropped it in 2007. It was a reasonably popular, well-understood policy and helped to demonstrate that publicly owned utilities served the people well.

On other occasions, however, lack of detailed process resulted in decisions that could have been improved, or better received by the public. An example of this was the decision made shortly before the 2007 election to promote a universal prescription drug plan that would extend the NDP's existing policy, of a fifteen dollar per prescription cap for seniors, to everyone.

Premier Calvert's quick planning failed to meet the arguments marshaled against the proposal. The concept of universal drug coverage is not bad or fiscally irresponsible as some portray it. Their arguments are basically the same arguments made by conservatives who tried to stop medicare from being introduced in the 1960s. The working poor and non-unionized people do not have the drug plans that the middle class enjoy. There are people who have to choose between medication and food for their kids.

The simple fact, for those who have a problem with the cost of such a plan, is that there is nothing offensive about the notion of everyone paying a bit more tax (if even required) to purchase pharmaceuticals in bulk, reduce existing private health plan premiums, lower drug costs, ensure everyone gets the medication they need, and to save on hospitalization costs. Either you believe in the value of this kind of social solidarity or you don't.

The problem with the plan, however, was that it was too quickly conceived and sprung on the public. It was decisive and bold, but because process was lacking, there had been no time to prepare the public and answer the critics. Thus, the NDP was on the defensive from the outset of the announcement of this plan early on in the 2007 election. Although a good concept, its promotion failed as a result of "back-of-the-envelope" planning.

Premier Calvert rarely imposed his will on cabinet and colleagues but wanted expedient decisions made. Where

Roy Romanow listened to the discussion and then defined the consensus before reaching a decision, Lorne Calvert's style was usually to allow discussion to go on until some consensus emerged, then make a decision at that moment. Both Lorne Calvert and his key advisors saw themselves as consensus builders, sometimes at the expense of providing needed direction, but still he managed to lead a well-intentioned and largely successful government.

Long-term service to government provided me with a rare opportunity to observe, close up, the different leadership styles of these two premiers and I can attest to their resilience and strength in their demanding roles of first minister.

Winning and Losing

WHEN YOU BECOME AN EXPERIENCED POLITICIAN, you develop a sixth sense that lets you anticipate election results with as much accuracy as any poll will provide. Sometimes the anticipation is confirmed by cumulative evidence; other times it is affirmed by a single significant event. Leading up to the 2003 election, the NDP was written off as a contender. Various media commentators and political analysts said it was "impossible" for the Calvert government to be re-elected. But my intuition told me something else.

More than one political scientist from the University of Saskatchewan shared the view that the NDP would inevitably be defeated in 2003. In fact, one of them, who had taught me thirty years before, had trouble believing me when I said I had been out canvassing, and my support was holding. NDP provincial treasurer Ken Rauch and ordinary citizens were telling me they hoped for and expected a return of the Calvert government. I actually increased my plurality and got over sixty-two percent of the vote in the 2003 election. Nevertheless, before the election, at least two political scientists I spoke to were very skeptical when I told them that there was support for the NDP. Apparently, not only are the experts not always right, but also you can't predict a political outcome until all the people have voted.

I advised my colleagues months before the election that, while it would be close, if we picked up a few percentage points of the vote from the New Green Alliance and a few percentage points from the Liberals, we had a chance. As a simple election strategy, I also felt we should tell the public what Elwin Hermanson and his MLA colleagues actually said on a day-to-day basis in the legislature. What they had to say was not, in my experience, in accord with mainstream Saskatchewan thinking. Simply put, they were too right wing. Their endless rants about crown corporations would imply to any thinking person that they wanted to get rid of them. Why else would they spend all their time complaining about them? If we could get this message to the public, it could damage the Saskatchewan Party's chances while it enhanced our own as protectors of the public's assets. By October 2003, a critical election question would be whether people would vote for the NDP because they wanted to leave the crown corporations intact.

During the 2003 election, in a media scrum, Elwin Hermanson refused to rule out selling off SaskTel and other crowns. This was a fatal mistake in political strategy from which he never recovered. I was serving on the NDP's election strategy team, which met each morning, in my case by telephone. When we heard his comment, we knew that Elwin had stumbled badly. Our strategy was reinforced and it immediately became clear that we would use his own words against him. Specifically, we decided we would use what he and others had said or were about to say about the ownership of crown corporations. We ordered new television and radio commercials that featured Elwin's own words. Though this strategy was somehow seen by the opposition and some media commentators as "dirty politics", we believed it was candid and appropriate. How can it be dirty politics to simply quote what someone says? Politicians should not expect that their statements in the legislature will not be raised at election time. If they feel free to attack crown corporations and their employees in the legislative assembly, often unfairly, often inaccurately, as was the case with the Saskatchewan Party, they should not be surprised when they are questioned about it later, or find their own words returning to haunt them.

NOW Communications, the NDP's public relations consultant, did a fantastic job for the party, clearly outperforming whoever came up with some of the Saskatchewan Party's simply weird and distracting 2003 election ads. The result was that the NDP gained ground daily, and what once was widely considered a given NDP defeat suddenly became a real election race.

We could see that the opposition was on the ropes as the campaign went on, as we watched the daily tracking polls. Especially telling was the televised leaders' debate, in which a well-prepared, calm, cool and collected Premier Lorne Calvert faced a sputtering, yelling, hectoring Elwin Hermanson, who did nothing to improve the position of the Saskatchewan Party by the time the cameras stopped.

The NDP win in 2003 was assisted by the recovering economy that, after enduring a few years of devastating drought, was slowly beginning to turn around. As well, the win was boosted by falling welfare numbers, better highways and lower income taxes — success stories that took away a lot of typical opposition ammunition. In fact, the Saskatchewan Party had actually stopped asking questions about these topics a few years before the election, which was a sign that these were no longer issues on which they could win votes.

In the end, the Saskatchewan Party stalled at thirty-eight percent of the vote. The voters clearly wanted the return of the NDP. And while many Sask Party members spent a lot of their energy after the campaign blaming the NDP's "dirty tricks" for their defeat, if any of them are still trying to figure out why they lost, they could start by looking in the mirror.

Having said that, I must add that they learned from their mistakes. Under new leader Brad Wall they, like Stephen Harper's Conservatives, kept most of their right-wing views to themselves, avoided controversy and went on to win the next election in 2007.

Serving on the NDP's strategy committee in the 2007 election, I found myself, once again, watching daily tracking polls. This time, however, the tables were turned. The Saskatchewan Party was on a roll, largely due to the fact that the NDP had been around for a long time. We saw events unfolding, and knew our job was not so much to retain government as to come up with an effective strategy to emerge with an eye to fighting another day.

Re-Shuffle and Start Again

AS I CAMPAIGNED FOR RE-ELECTION IN 2003 in the new Saskatoon Massey Place Constituency, I canvassed a man on Avenue P who owned a small business. He asked me what I hoped to accomplish if returned to the legislature, which is a very good question for any voter to ask a politician. I replied that I had promised in 1999 that I would work to implement a new personal income tax system, and that was done. I was now minister of Industry and Resources as well as Justice, and my main priority would be to work to make those changes that could be made to encourage economic development and job growth. I reminded him that we had started with the royalty changes for oil and gas, and mining changes to encourage exploration and prospecting, as well as encouraging capital investment in the potash sector. What more could be done? I said that is what I wanted to continue to work on, as well as a thorough examination of business taxation.

In reflecting on my answer to that voter, I realized that members of the legislature have differing priorities, and that is a good thing. For me, tax and economic issues came to occupy my time, even though I really didn't expect them to. Other members lend their expertise to different pressing matters. Peter Prebble, for example, was ever watchful about social services and social justice issues. He is also, of course, a dedicated environmentalist. Though I disagreed with Peter about his approach to several issues, I respected him and the work he did. He brought a knowledge and enthusiasm to the NDP that allowed us to work together for the public interest.

Others bring their individual strengths to the table. Buckley Belanger brings the invaluable perspective of aboriginal people and northerners to government. Judy Junor's nursing background is very useful where health matters are concerned. In almost every case, MLAs bring experience, skill and interest in one or more areas. As in any complex organization, government requires collaborative effort and management of personal motivations to achieve the collective good.

Given my desire to continue in Industry and Resources, I was happy on election night to see Frank Quennell elected in Saskatoon Meewasin. I suspected that the premier would ask him to become minister of Justice and Attorney General, since the only other two lawyers in government, John Nilson and I, had already been there. I also felt, with some justification, that I had developed a credibility and rapport with the business community as Finance minister and, for some months, as minister of Industry and Resources, and could continue the work I had begun in that area.

There was some speculation that Premier Calvert would ask me to resume my duties at Finance, since Finance Minister Jim Melenchuk had, unfortunately, been defeated. I thought, however, that this was unlikely, since once you have been there you don't normally go back. Furthermore, I thought the public might want a new face in the position. I'd had my opportunity to make some changes, and it was someone else's turn.

Since being elected in 1991, I had never offered my opinion to either Premier Romanow or Premier Calvert as to what I thought they should do when it came to naming cabinet ministers. The selection of a cabinet is the sole prerogative of a prime minister or premier. In this one instance, they have the right to do whatever they want, although most would know that their choices are critical to a well-functioning government.

Of course, they, too, are subject to many pressures. It is an incredibly difficult task. Egos are involved. Feelings are hurt. Some become "ins". Some are demoted. Some remain "outs". All have ambitions. So, it is a very difficult decision for any premier as the self-esteem, spirit and confidence of elected party members can hang in the balance. What further complicates the decision is that the premier has to have a cabinet that not only brings skills to the table, but also duly represents genders, various regions, different races, religions, age groups, interests and other factors.

Once, when Roy Romanow was in the process of putting together one of his cabinets and was being fairly harassed by the MLAs, he said, "If any of you are considering providing me with advice on how to make up the cabinet — don't."

I never offered any premier advice unless asked and, when approached for a cabinet position, was simply informed the day before what responsibilities I was to take on.

Thus, after the defeat of Jim Melenchuk, I didn't offer Premier Calvert any advice on who I thought should be appointed minister of Finance. If he would have asked me, however, I would have advised him to appoint Harry Van Mulligan, a veteran Regina MLA who had earlier been dropped from cabinet after serving as Social Services minister. I knew Harry to be a solid and able individual and knew that he had a good grasp of fiscal issues. In fact, Premier Calvert did ask Harry to fill the role, and I was happy to remain as vice-chair of Treasury Board. I had also served in that capacity when Jim Melenchuk succeeded me as Finance minister.

Being minister of Finance is a tough job and if I could play a supportive role to my successors, I was happy to do so. Working with Harry Van Mulligan would make it all that much easier. As well, the Department of Justice was in the good hands of Frank Quennell, who proved to be a very thoughtful and able minister. Given these appointments after the 2003 election, I thought that I would remain in familiar territory, continuing with my work in Industry and Resources, and assisting where my experience might be of some use. However, you never know what is on the premier's mind following an election.

Double Duty

EITHER PREMIER LORNE CALVERT LIKED ME OR he didn't like me, because he gave me enough work and responsibility to keep me very busy, and my job description seemed to grow by paragraphs. Along with being minister of Industry and Resources, minister responsible for the Saskatchewan Research Council, minister responsible for the Saskatchewan Opportunities Corporation (Research Parks), the Saskatchewan Government Growth Fund and the Information Services Corporation, I served as vice-chair of Treasury Board and a member of the Crown Management Board (the holding company for the crown corporations). And just in case I had a few spare hours, he made me minister responsible for the new and controversial Investment Saskatchewan and asked that I assume responsibility for the sometimes difficult and controversial Saskatchewan Liquor and Gaming Authority (SLGA), as well as Tourism Saskatchewan.

Eight primary roles and two additional board appointments were a lot of responsibility, but, I like to be kept busy. It was the way I had always been deployed in government. My years as Health minister, Finance minister, and dual roles as minister of Industry and Resources/minister of Justice and Attorney General had always kept me fully engaged, and had prepared me for anything that a premier might request of me.

As premiers often do, Lorne gave me some instructions as to certain tasks he wanted done in some of these roles. Of course, I agreed to his instructions and carried them out. He was the premier, and if you can't accept the instructions with a resolve to do them, don't take the job.

As the public can attest, a particularly hot portfolio was the Liquor and Gaming Authority. It had some weighty challenges and I felt that it would be a handful. However, I learned quickly that, at least, the Authority staff was competent and dedicated. Headed by President Sandra Morgan, a veteran of legislative and public service, Sandra was someone I already knew, and for whom I had a high regard. After being sworn in as SLGA minister at Government House, I immediately drove to her office and began to meet with the staff.

Issues abounded at SLGA. What would be done about the Federation of Saskatchewan Indian Nations' proposal for a casino outside of Saskatoon? Nothing gets more controversial in Saskatoon politics than casino-related issues. What about a proposed Swift Current casino, recently endorsed by the people of Swift Current in a referendum? How would we deal with the rather thorny questions arising from the provincial auditor's reports on the casinos already operated by the Saskatchewan Indian Gaming Authority (SIGA)? Extravagant spending by former SIGA CEO Dutch Lerat had led to his departure from SIGA. But there were also many recommendations for improved accountability that were not yet complied with. There was a lot more work to be done and it would all be under public scrutiny. While these audit issues were ongoing, the proposal for a new casino on the Whitecap Dakota First Nation had to be decided. I stated publicly that it would not be approved until the recommendations of the provincial auditor were complied with. Ultimately, they were, after much effort by both SIGA and SLGA.

In August 2004, I recommended to cabinet that the Saskatoon-area casino be approved. This initiative of moving the Dakota Dunes project to completion and bringing the auditor's recommendations into force helped stabilize the First Nations' casino enterprises in the province. It was a good beginning and alleviated some of my misgivings about this hot portfolio.

At least, as minister of the Saskatchewan Liquor and Gaming Authority, I didn't have to worry about our policy on whether or not to privatize the government-owned liquor stores, since both the NDP and the public had made their views quite clear. They did not want privatization. Neither did I. For most of the public it is often not known, or else conveniently forgotten, that much of liquor distribution in Saskatchewan is already in private hands. While there are eighty-one government-owned liquor stores, there are over 190 private franchisees in small centres selling liquor, and over 400 "off-sale" outlets selling beer. There are private beer and wine stores, and hotels are allowed to sell spirits.

To put the matter in perspective, about 56% of the beer sold in Saskatchewan is sold by private "off-salers", about 28% is sold by government liquor stores, and another 16% sold privately through franchisees, restaurants and lounges. It is untrue to say that government controls all liquor and beer sales, although the Canadian Taxpayers' Federation and sometimes the Saskatchewan Party will likely continue to leave that impression. But thankfully, it was not the issue that

I thought it could have been when I inherited the portfolio. And while there were other contentious issues, as one would expect in such a portfolio, most of the work went smoothly. By the time Deb Higgins replaced me as minister responsible for Liquor and Gaming in February 2006, I believe I had accomplished the work the premier wished me to undertake in that role.

After the cabinet shuffle in 2003, each of my inherited new responsibilities brought its own challenges, and each required dedicated planning to evoke strategies that would best serve the people of Saskatchewan. Some, such as my term as chair of the Liquor and Gaming Authority required me to pay great attention to my own backyard of Saskatoon. Some of these new challenges led me to speak at the World Nuclear Association Symposium in London, UK. Others would lead me to head trade delegations on energy resources and biotechnology to the United States. No matter what the task was, I always tried to focus on the need to move forward through economic development and job creation for Saskatchewan people, especially youth. No matter how many years you serve in government, if you are not ready for new engagements, you are there for the wrong reasons.

That Zany Vancouver Sense Of Humour

IN FEBRUARY 2007, I WAS SENT TO VANCOUVER, along with business people and Industry and Resources staff, as part of the "Innovative by Nature" campaign. This was designed to target business investors and prospective new residents with positive messages about Saskatchewan's economy. It was an intelligent campaign that resonated well.

Business people were very receptive to the message that the Saskatchewan economy was innovative, strong and diversified, and that there were good investment opportunities to be had. Investment was already growing in Saskatchewan, but the campaign was designed to build on that momentum. And, many people who had moved away from Saskatchewan were eager to consider new job opportunities that might allow them to move back home.

One of the ideas department staff came up with was to offer the BC public a trip for two to the Junos, to be held in Saskatoon in early April 2007. So they gave the tickets to Philip Till, of CKNW Vancouver Radio. Philip Till turned out to be a crusty talk show host. He was a successor to Jack Webster, and had the largest talk show audience in

Canada. He took the opportunity to create a contest whereby listeners had to complete the sentence "You know you're in Saskatchewan when . . ." Of course, with Philip's sarcastic encouragement, the latte-drinking and rain-drenched people of the lower mainland used the opportunity to poke fun at Saskatchewan, employing every stereotypical cliché about our fair province.

"You know you're in Saskatchewan when you fill up your pick-up and it immediately doubles in value." "You know you're in Saskatchewan when your dog runs away and you can see it for three days." And so on.

I went on the talk show one Thursday morning and told Philip a few things he needed to know about Saskatchewan, which, after all, was by then a "have" province, unlike British Columbia at the time. I had no idea that my five or ten minutes of fame on this show, and the contest, would cause such a brouhaha in Saskatchewan.

All that day, in Vancouver, local people I met told me that they had heard me on the radio show and thought I'd done really well answering Philip. I was surprised when I called my office and was told that CTV was doing a story on the contest, and other media were interested, too. By the time I got back to Saskatoon the next day, all the radio stations were talking about it, and making fun of Vancouverites. At least three of them had their own "You know you're in Vancouver when . . . " contests going on, and everyone was talking about it in the coffee shops and around the water coolers.

I thought it was hilarious, and said so at a big media scrum in Saskatoon. The Saskatchewan Party, of course, was "outraged". Brad Wall had already demanded we rescind the offer of the tickets, and Don Morgan joined him in letting the world know how irresponsible and incompetent I was to allow people to actually poke fun at us.

But, no one really agreed with them. People were having a good time poking fun at the people of Vancouver. And, it was noted that a lot of people were actually talking about Saskatchewan in BC, as well as rallying around Saskatchewan in Saskatchewan. They were telling everyone about our lower cost of living, affordable housing, sunshine, and so on. Any time you can get people to count their blessings, it's a good thing.

Ron Petrie of the *Regina Leader-Post* wrote a column, which contained some pretty good lines. Among others, he wrote: "you know you're in British Columbia when . . .

• Your province's No. 1 agricultural export is sold not by the bushel, but by the quarter-ounce.

• Your driving directions to any point in the city include, as landmarks, at least five Starbucks, three hookers and two heroin aficionados.

• Your only hope for one day getting ahead of the interest payments and securing some equity in your retirement cottage is brought to you by the letters B and B.

• Just one more traffic bridge and your largest city will trail Saskatoon by only three.

• You walk four blocks to a corner store during the sixth consecutive day of rain for a bottle of imported water.

There is something completely worthwhile in getting people engaged in provincial pride, and in a year when Saskatchewan had bragging rights for the Rider's win at the Grey Cup, Saskatchewan people could now also point to our economy with real self-esteem and say to the rest of Canada — "We have arrived!"

Keeping The Faith

WHILE ATTENDING PERSEPHONE THEATRE IN SASKATOON with our neighbours and friends, Rick and Linda Ewen, Pauline and I were standing in the crowded lobby when a guy came up to me and loudly told me what a disastrous job he thought the government and I were doing. Rick and Linda were a bit perturbed and thought that this should not happen on a social outing. I said that you just had to accept that that sort of thing would happen from time to time. If you can't put up with it, then you shouldn't be in politics. I have certainly dished out criticism of my political opponents on occasion, so I have to expect to take it, too.

The people of Saskatchewan, of all political stripes, are good and decent people. Many words and acts of kindness were extended to me throughout my political career. Like most people, I get down and discouraged on occasion. And it was sometimes strangers who came up to me on the street and said encouraging words like: "You're doing a good job" or "I appreciate the work you do" or words to that effect. I don't know if people realize how much it means to others to receive a few words of encouragement in a world where we sometimes just don't hear them often. On a few occasions when I'd had enough and been ready to throw in the towel, I would run into someone who encouraged me and completely turned me around. I am sure others have had similar experiences in their lives. I try to remember to tell people how much I appreciate knowing them, or what they do, but I am sure I don't do it enough.

Small, passing incidents or a few simple words can often change the course of our lives. We are glad when we affect people positively, when we "shine" as human beings. Most of us have also done or said things, which, on reflection, we wish we hadn't. The very nature of living creates many moments when we have a choice in how we affect others, and no matter who we are or where we have come from, we must remember that.

My father was an alcoholic and, as most children of alcoholics know, they sometimes lash out at others, probably because of their own frustration and as a result of hurt they have endured themselves. In my dad's case, I am sure that four years of World War II, participation in the disastrous Dieppe Raid, tuberculosis and fifteen years of cancer had a lot to do with it. As well, like many fathers of his generation, he did not give me any words of encouragement directly. One day, though, I overheard him talking to one of his drinking buddies. I was in the next room.

"I think Eric will go far because he is honest and he is dedicated," he said. I was quite surprised because I didn't particularly think of myself in those terms and I had no idea he had a good opinion of me. These words had a big impact. For the first time in my life, I actually started to believe that maybe I could do something.

My mother, on the other hand, was very open with words of kindness and praise. A powerful memory comes back to me repeatedly. I am about five years old, and I am standing on a city sidewalk looking up into the kitchen window of a house a few blocks from where we lived. My mother is in the kitchen washing dishes. She is going to this house every day to make meals and look after these five kids that live there. But they are not her kids. At home, she has six kids, and I can't understand why my mother is going to their house to take care of them instead of staying home and taking care of us.

In fact, she didn't even know these people. This was the house of a man who had been hired to paint our kitchen. He was the man whose daughter had been hit by a car while crossing the street. She was in the hospital and her mother was with her day after day. My mother went into this home to help out, because it was the right thing to do.

As I grew older and this memory returned to me repeatedly, I came to understand and appreciate it. As an adult, I ran into other people who had relayed incidents to me of how my parents had helped them out. Sometimes, I remembered these incidents, and sometimes I knew nothing about them.

When my mother died in 1986, one of my aunts wrote to me and said that my mother had a "wonderful ministry". At first, I thought that this was an odd choice of words, since my mother wasn't a minister. Then I thought about it and realized that it is not up to the priests and ministers to do all that needs to be done. It is the job of each of us to contribute and to minister to the needs of others, as best we can, according to our abilities. The clergy are just the cheerleaders who encourage us to do so.

I think I went into politics to try to help out in some way. I hope that, on an individual basis, I have helped some people when they needed it, made a difference and perhaps encouraged them in a way that may help them encourage someone else. On a wider level, I hope some of the work I have done will advance my province, and provide greater opportunities.

In my first speech in the Legislature in December 1991, I said that I had come there to represent my neighbours. I ended my remarks by saying that I hoped I would not break faith with them. I hope I have maintained their trust. I also hope that those who come after me will not break faith with the people.

For many months leading up to December 2006, I increasingly felt that my days of elected politics were coming to an end. I had little personal time and, over the years, had not devoted the time to Pauline and my family that I should have. It is my biggest regret. Years of constant meetings, and community and public events, which occupied most evenings and weekends, made me long for more private and family time.

As well, I wanted to challenge myself to establish a new career, preferably in the private sector in Saskatoon. But knowing what I would do next would have to wait until I was no longer minister of Industry and Resources. Otherwise I would be in a conflict of interest. I felt I was still young enough and energetic enough to embark on a third career. It was time to reinvent myself.

I also had to admit to myself that there were no burning political or economic issues I wanted to resolve. Certainly, there continue to be many ongoing problems that politicians in Saskatchewan and elsewhere must face, but none that I felt would need me to be the lead player. It was time to make way for someone new, to renew our party and to give a younger person an opportunity to serve. My time as a politician was done.

So, on December 15, 2006, I sat beside Premier Calvert at a Saskatoon news conference, and announced I would not run in the next provincial election. I said it was a time for self-renewal, political renewal and professional renewal. I complimented Premier Calvert and the government on the job being done. I thanked my wife, constituents, supporters, my constituency assistants, Lynda MacPherson, Treena Dobson and Donna Rederburg, my ministerial staff, constituency executive, legislative colleagues and the public service. I was able to sum up sixteen years in a few short paragraphs that truly reflect the way I feel about the whole experience:

There is, justifiably, great optimism for the future of our province.

The governments which I have been associated with since 1991 have built a strong foundation of good public policy, fiscal soundness, and tax competitiveness which will serve the people of Saskatchewan well.

When our party came to power in 1991, Saskatchewan was nearly bankrupt, underemployed and in despair.

I have seen that despair replaced by hope, from which a general feeling of confidence has, now, emerged.

Thank you, to all concerned, for allowing me to play a small part in that turnaround, and best wishes for continued progress.

Life is a journey for each of us. For a time my journey took me down a political road. Walking down that road was a pleasure, because I always walked alongside others who shared the adventure.